THE BUSINESS REVIVAL

GETTING WHAT IS INSIDE OF YOU INSIDE OF YOUR WORKPLACE

D. BRANDON HAIRE

WITH DREW STEADMAN

THE BUSINESS REVIVAL

Published by Clear Day Publishing, a division of Clear Day Media Group LLC, Waco, TX, cleardaypublishing.com.

Published in association with Lux Creative {theluxcreative.com}

Unless otherwise noted, Scripture quotations are taken from the New American Standard Bible®, Copyright © 1960, 1962, 1963, 1968, 1971, 1972, 1973, 1975, 1977, 1995 by The Lockman Foundation. Used by permission. (www.Lockman.org)

Quotations designated NIV are from The Holy Bible, New International Version®, NIV® Copyright © 1973, 1978, 1984, 2011 by Biblica, Inc.® Used by permission. All rights reserved worldwide.

Quotations designated NKJV are taken from the New King James Version®. Copyright © 1982 by Thomas Nelson, Inc. Used by permission. All rights reserved.

Quotations designated ESV are taken from The Holy Bible, English Standard Version® (ESV®) Copyright © 2001 by Crossway, a publishing ministry of Good News Publishers. All rights reserved. ESV Text Edition: 2011

ISBN: 978-1-7326252-5-9
Library of Congress Control Number: 2020942812

Cover Design: Carolynn Seibert
Interior Design: Lux Creative {theluxcreative.com}

Printed in the United States of America.

CONTENTS

FOREWORD

It is a privilege to write the foreword for *The Business Revival* and to provide a few short pastoral perspectives throughout the book. I met Brandon shortly after he moved to Waco with his wife and newborn son. He had recently left a lucrative position in banking and was in the midst of a difficult career change. We quickly connected like old friends and have remained close ever since. Through walking with Brandon during these years, I have received an inside view into a powerful move of God.

I have heard many Christian intellectuals lament the divide between the sacred and the secular as they theorize what it might look like for believers to live an integrated spiritual life. I've read and listened to more teachings about "Kingdom business" than I can count. I've sat through various evangelism and discipleship trainings, many targeted at people in the workplace, focused on cutting edge techniques.

Unfortunately, for as much theory I've learned, I have not heard many stories of these ideals being realized in real life. The few stories I've heard tend to be examples of entrepreneurs. I have celebrated what God did in these companies but have struggled to understand how a person who didn't own a business or work in the C-Suite could do the same. What does "Kingdom business" look like for a retail clerk or entry level salesperson? Perhaps you are asking the same question.

Most Christians agree that Christians should live an integrated life, that who they are on Monday is just as important as who they are on Sunday. But what does it mean to actually live "on mission"? There are a wide range of opinions: Does God commission believers in the workplace primarily so they might evangelize? Or is their responsibility to live as witnesses by their Christ-like character? Or perhaps Christians in the workplace are meant to change corporate culture from within to be more humane and people-focused? Or is the nature of work itself a redeemed act that reflects the Creator? I've heard compelling arguments for all the above, yet all seem incomplete.

In *Business Revival*, you will certainly see elements of each of the above, but it cannot be reduced to any one of them. Furthermore, it is not fundamentally a story of human activity. If you ask Brandon, he will answer simply: The key is prayer. At one level, there is more to it—learning to love difficult people, endurance, boldness, and more. But it truly is all about prayer. Prayer is the critical act because God is the primary actor. A business revival is not about human technique; instead, it's about God showing up and moving through willing people.

When God shows up, things change. Whole families surrender to Jesus for the first time. Marriages are restored. People start living with integrity in their business dealings. The culture of the department starts to change to prioritize people over profits (which, ironically, often leads to more profits)! Prayer acknowledges this reality by contending for God to move in ways that only He can.

This business revival started with prayer. In fact, for nearly two years that is all that happened. You won't find a silver bullet evangelistic or management technique in this book. Instead, you will read that two men faithfully interceded every single week for their company while they worked diligently to hit their sales goals. They didn't recognize it at first, but God was moving. I slowly started to hear testimonies of people encountering God. It started to dawn on us all that God was moving in a powerful way.

Now, more than seven years later, Brandon regularly shares testimonies with me of people receiving Jesus, experiencing healing, and relationships being restored. Just yesterday he texted me with another powerful salvation story. They have now seen more than one hundred people receive Christ and enter into discipleship relationships. Prayer groups have started to emerge in various companies around the nation as former employees move on to different jobs. I know many of the employees in Brandon's department and have watched the whole culture change. They perform at a high level, and they do so from a place of putting people first. It is a holistic witness to the Kingdom of God. And it all started with prayer.

More than the stories of revival, I am honored to write the foreword because I consider Brandon to be a close friend and a true brother in Christ. I am far more impressed by his personal integrity, walk with God, and who he is as a father and a husband than I am with his business success. I could say the same for many of the other people I know who work in his department.

I pray that these stories inspire you to love Jesus, to seek Him first in every aspect of your life, and to gather a few others to pray for your workplace. You will be disappointed if you are looking for a step-by-step guide to revival; instead, read these pages to discover a real story about real people experiencing a real God in the midst of a real business. Let these stories fill your heart with faith and let's believe together for revival fires to be ignited in countless workplaces throughout our nation and our world.

Drew Steadman, July 2020

INTRODUCTION

NOW WHAT DO I DO?

I used to think the best business lessons came from experience;
now I know they come from parenting too.

This book begins with a revelation I received only ten days ago.
My wife and son(s) have come up to the office almost every Wednesday to have lunch with me. The older boys have grown and are in
school, so these days it's normally just my youngest son who visits the
office. On this particular Wednesday, our oldest son was home from
school after recovering from a recent illness, so he joined his younger
brother in visiting Daddy's work.

"Hey bud, you want to tell Daddy what you told me about
school?" My wife motioned to our oldest.

"No, ma'am." He shook her off.

"What happened, bud?" I replied as I unboxed my chicken
nuggets.

I could see the tenderness rush over him like goosebumps, as he
began to tell me that some boys are mean to him on the playground
when they play football. I carefully asked him to tell me more and
listened intently. Though I wanted to say, "What are their daddy's
names, where do they work, and you know your daddy is pretty
advanced in Tae Kwon Do right?" I knew this was a time to listen.
"Listen to me, Hunter. There will be tons of times in your life where
men will be jealous of you and feel less than around you. They will try
to pick on you because YOU ARE AMAZING in so many things!
I continued to affirm my son and asked more questions to decipher
reality. As we finished, I looked at my son, who now had tears in his
eyes.

"Hunter, what's up bud? Is there more?"

"No, Daddy. These are just happy tears. No one talks to me the way you do when I am sad. You know just how to make me feel better."

With a quick rush of emotions, I wrapped my arms around my boy and continued to tell him who he is. As they walked to the car to leave, I continued to pour affirmation and truth over my son.

Once the car pulled away, I marched right back inside. I started Googling everything I could imagine: "How to teach children to properly throw and catch." "Make football fun." "What age does coordination really show?" I was determined to teach my son to compete.

As I pulled into the driveway that evening, my wife and sons greeted me at the door and Hunter asked the greatest question on the planet:

"Hey, dad, you want to throw the football?"

Oh, you bet your life I do! Until my arm falls off and Mama has to drag me inside. All my high school glory days on the field came rushing back over me like a wave. I changed my work clothes like superman in a phone booth, and we were both outside in a flash. As we threw the ball back and forth, he caught every pass and then threw it back with a perfect spiral.

"Go deeper, buddy." I waved him backwards.

More of the same. He caught every single pass and threw the ball back well. I was impressed and couldn't figure out the flaw in his game. It forced me to ask more questions. "How do your buddies throw it?" "Are they long passes?" "High passes?" "Hard throws?" I was baffled. Hunter caught every type of throw I threw his way.

"Hunter, come here for a second."

"Yes, sir?"

"When do your friends get angry and yell at you during football? You have caught twenty passes in a row and Daddy was throwing some of them hard."

"Well, when I catch the ball, they scream, 'Run Hunter! Gosh! Go! What are you doing?!'"

The cause of the problem suddenly hit me.

"Buddy, do you not know what to do after you catch the ball?" I softened.

"No, sir." He smiled.

Hunter and I had been playing "catch" for years, but I simply had not taught him what to do with the ball after he caught it. Within thirty minutes, we were inside drawing plays, while I explained players, positions, and rules. He picked it up instantly; in fact, he started to create his own plays.

This is exactly what it is like for most believers. We go to church, we know the scriptures, we pray over our food, we send missionaries to faraway places, but we don't know what to do Monday morning in our workplaces. How can I make a living and a difference? How is this place of work my mission field? I don't feel called to Africa so does that mean I can't participate in God's Purpose?

I pray this book ignites the embers smoldering inside of you— that a passion and a sense of purpose would emerge for where you already are. It is my hope that you would take the Sunday catch and turn it into Monday touchdowns in the game of life you are already playing. After years of ministering in my workplace, I've found many Christians are like my son; they desire to make a difference but do not know how to run nor make the plays. We "catch" the best sermons, see the newest Christian film, even have Christian friends, but we do not know how to translate this into life-changing moments. How do we pray for the co-worker battling cancer or bring salvation moments to the hardest people to love in our workplace? How can we take a sermon to our co-worker who has been trying to get pregnant for a decade?

In this book, I want to walk you through personal stories of success, honor, failure, hope, and challenge to show you the playbook. *Business Revival* is my personal journey, including the outside perspective of one of my closest friends and longtime pastor Drew Steadman. It is about the strength to step in and step up into your current role. This book will give you strength and hope to press forward. In the global society in which we are all living and breathing, we are told to look out for number one and to quit if things are hard. We are told that Sunday is for church, where we perform like everyone else and sit in the back row not to be noticed. However, I have tasted and seen that the truest form of fulfillment in the business world is to get what is INSIDE you INSIDE your workplace. Let these stories and pastoral perspectives shape, challenge, and drive you into a life and world you never knew was possible.

LET'S START TO BELIEVE FOR REVIVAL

RETAIL PASTOR

*I used to think pastors preached their best sermons on Sunday;
now I know they save the best for their side hustle.*

I can still hear the shuffle of his scuffed SAS shoes against the hundred-year-old wood floors, and the sound of his made-up gospel songs creep through my mind to this day. The peace, love, and joy revealed through his every move could be felt by everyone visiting the store. His name was Billy Pedigo. Or Bill. Or Brother Billy as customers called him. Bill was a pastor at a small church in town, but he also held a second job at a department store for his "play money." This is where I met the "real" Bill. Even though he was almost fifty years older than me, he had an infectious laugh and youthfulness that kept me on my toes. There were days of stocking heavy boxes where my sole goal was to keep up with Brother Billy. That man knew how to work!

The retail store was a good job for me during my college years. It worked around my school schedule, paid pretty good commission, and hired me back after returning from China. This was a place where I spent six days a week for almost seven years of my life. Bill was there the entire time. He and I spent a lot of life together in during that time period. We broke bread together, we cried together, and laughed a lot. We were close, not just co-workers. So much so, that I remember the tears falling down his face when I asked him to officiate my wedding. He was a man that I admired in more ways than I can write.

Almost ninety percent of our job was selling men's dress shoes and cowboy boots as commissioned salespeople. This led to many friendly competitions. When I am in my seventies, I hope my competitive side is as alive and well as his was. Bill and I turned everything into a competition. Who can sell the most? Stock the fastest? Eat the most sausage wraps from the BBQ joint next door? Kill the most bugs? But in all the fun and laughs, there was one record neither one of us wanted: the most boots tried on the same customer *without* closing the sale. This is what the death of a commission check looks like. Too many records like this one, and the creative ramen noodle chef is born.

I can remember the day Bill broke this record. Bill often used an old-timer salesman's trick where he walked to the glass doors to "look at what the weather was doing." When a customer walked in, he was there to open the door and politely ask, "Can I help you with something?" Then without fail, he would grin in my direction when they replied, "Just looking for boots." This day was no exception. Bill leaned behind the counter, pulled out his black plastic comb, combed his gray hair straight back and paused.

"I think I am going to go see what the weather is doing, Brandon."

"Okay, Bill." My face grimaced. "How does he always beat me to it?" I mumbled.

As the scent of Bill's aftershave wafted across the old wooden floors, a well-dressed gentleman glided through the glass doors.

"Can I help you, sir?" Bill's deep voice bellowed.

"Yes, what kind of *Lucchese* boots do you sell?"

For those of you that have no clue what this man was asking for, he had basically walked into the store and said, "Can I spend anywhere between five-hundred and a couple thousand bucks, please?" Needless to say, this broke salesman was playfully irritated with "Brother Billy" for beating me to the customer. As Bill guided the gentleman to the blue leather chairs, I begged God to see a hurting twenty-three-year-old salesman in need of commission. Instead, God saw a customer in need of compassion. While I was trapped in my *why not me* attitude, Bill started with the usual: "What brings you in today?" The gentleman shrugged off the question and stood per-plexed in front of the massive boot display wall. I watched him look at every exotic boot we carried. Just about the time the man asked to try on his first pair of boots, another customer walked in and headed straight for the boots. I asked the second gentleman if I could help, and he said, "Yep, I need two pair of these in size 10D, and I don't need to try 'em on either."

I hopped back into the stock room with an attitude towards my competitor and returned to ring up the much cheaper boots for my customer. Another couple walked in and asked for a specific, one hundred-dollar boot. Again, I obliged. Third sale complete. With the cockiest of grins dancing across my face, I looked over at Bill and counted the numerous different boxes on the ground. My friend was a little out of breath, yet he was more focused than I had seen in a long time. I caught the phrase, *"I am so sorry to hear that..."* several times.

On Bill's next trip back to the stock room, I followed to see if I could help and get the scoop. As Bill caught his breath, I climbed the ladder to fetch another size and asked what was going on. Bill proceeded to tell me that the gentleman was in town to attend his mother's funeral. He had not spoken to her in twenty years. Once I handed Bill the new boot box, he grinned proudly and winked.

"God is up to something today, Brandon."

My first thought was that Bill's blood-sugar might be low because it sure seemed like the only thing God was up to was punishing a pastor. In my mind, this guy was trying on a ton of shoes and my friend was stuck listening to his grief. All the while, I was making sales and commissions to pay my bills. However, as my preacher friend charged forward, I was intrigued enough to stay at a distance and watch. Three more customers came in at different times looking for boots while Bill continued to talk with the gentleman. Three completed sales for me, none for Bill. At one point, there were so many boots scattered across the floor that my customers couldn't get to the display wall. In all of the back and forth, my friend stayed consistent and spoke to the man with complete gentleness.

"Bill, can I help put some of these boots away for you guys?" I tried to help.

As Bill nodded and pointed to a section of boots stacked high, I glanced up at the man's face. His eyes were blood-shot and the salt from his tears had made two perfect lines down his cheeks. In the midst of the boot box counting, I tried to hear more of the conversation. Finally, I was down to the last four boxes. Bill lifted himself from the foot stool and walked beside the man. With the two of them walking to the register, I noticed my friend holding a pair of five-dollar socks.

"Bill, you guys need any of these?" I pointed to the remaining boots.

"No Hun, we are all set." He held up the socks.

I was starting to grow infuriated on behalf of my friend. All that time and no sale? As I walked back to the stockroom with the last three boxes, I finished counting...fifty-one...fifty-two...fifty-three. The previous record was twenty-nine. I know because it was mine. (Somewhere out there, a shoe salesperson is reading this and they are weeping.) As my heels clicked along the long tile hallway, I looked up to see Bill bear-hugging this crying man. Bill was praying. There was a gentleness and compassion pouring from my friend that caused my eyes to water. After the hug, the man quickly wiped his face, grabbed his black socks, and headed out the door.

"What was that all about?" I shrugged.

"That was about meeting someone in their spot in life, not fancy boots." Bill grinned.

"I mean, what happened?" I persisted.

As Bill began to unfold the man's story in detail, we both turned to the sound of that very man's heels clomping towards us. Instantly, I looked back at the blue chairs to see if the gentleman might have forgotten something.

"Could I ask you one more thing?" The man marched straight for Bill.

"Sure, Tom."

"Where does all that come from—I mean there is something different in you." Tom pointed at Bill.

"That's easy. It's my faith in my Lord, Jesus," Bill responded with his easy southern drawl.

Then within a matter of seconds, Tom asked three more questions to follow-up his question. I was fortunate enough to be standing right next to Bill as he walked Tom back over to the blue chairs. I tagged along without saying a word. I had seen him pray over people in our store several times, but this was a whole new conversation. Like a small child waiting for ice cream, I could not take my eyes off the two men. The gentleman was asking a lot of the questions while my friend sat listening, asked clarifying questions if needed, and then calmly responded to each. I kept waiting for the question every Sunday school Christian would have been waiting for: "Tom, if you died today, would you go to Heaven or Hell?" But with each passing question about God, my pastor friend calmly and patiently loved the man in front of him by listening with the intent to understand, not listening with the intent to respond.

As the short conversation continued, the store remained customer-free and I stayed glued to the answers from Bill.

"What do I do, Bill?" Tom raised his hands.

"What do you mean, Tom?"

"I mean, I can't keep living like this—bitter, angry, and hurting everyone." He began to cry.

"Tom, that bitterness in you is like drinking poison and hoping everyone else gets sick. It won't do you any good." Bill leaned in towards Tom.

In a matter of seconds, Tom began to weep and asked my friend to help him get rid of his bitterness. Bill gently placed his massive hands on Tom's bowed head and told him, "I can't take that bitterness, but I know the one who can."

That day my friend, Brother Billy, led a man to Jesus, and he did it with patience, understanding, and love. He served him to the point of frustration and exhaustion. He brought him comfort. He gently addressed his heart. Then he passionately prayed. By the time Tom left our store, Bill's nice dress shirt was covered with his snot and tears. However, a wounded man experienced a new taste of healing. Within a few minutes after the glass door slammed closed, Bill and I were standing silently folding new stock clothes. As we stacked the items neatly into each cube, Bill paused and grinned.

"So, how many boots did he try on?"

"53." I busted into laughter. It was a new record.

I learned something profound that day: let God use you right where you are. We don't have to go on a mission trip to be used greatly by God. If we are faithful in the place where God has placed us, he can't help but use us. The gentleman that Bill helped that day needed someone to meet him where he was and to love him with no strings attached. No commission needed. The greatest question each one of us can ask ourselves is this: What am I here for and who am I here for? Can you imagine what your days would look like if you started them with this question?

The most valuable piece of learning I received from Bill, day in and day out, was to simply let God flow through you. I had served as a missionary in China and even wrote a book about the story yet Bill was reaching the multitudes just the same. I didn't have to memorize every Scripture to let the love and light of Jesus flow through me. I didn't even have to charge up to every customer with gospel tracks. This, in my opinion, is exactly what the typical Christian thinks "God with you at work" is about.

The Business Revival happens from a life and lifestyle pointing to Jesus. Bill was a Pastor yes, but more importantly, he was a faithful employee and an ambassador for Christ no matter where he was. His knowledge of the Bible, his preaching, and his teaching didn't show the love of Christ like his life did. When you show up to work knowing that Jesus is showing up with you, then lives will be changed and a revival will happen in your workplace. Bill's example challenged me and motivated me. I realized I was called into this lifestyle of witness just as much as he was. Years later, after leaving banking and moving into a new career, I remembered Bill and sought to follow in his footsteps.

PASTORAL PERSPECTIVE: IDENTITY AND PURPOSE

What does it mean to be a Christian businessperson? I've heard this question quite a bit in my years of pastoral ministry. At one level, it's not a bad question. After all, we should take our calling seriously. But what are people actually asking?

For some people, this is primarily a question of *validation* as they grapple with how their nine-to-five fits within God's purposes. Perhaps they imagine a type of heavenly pecking order with missionaries at the top, followed by doctors, pastors, and teachers—businesspeople somewhere in the middle, depending on industry, and lawyers rounding out the bottom of the list. Our *career* gets wrapped up with our *identity* in this imagination. And it completely warps the conversation. If we fall into this trap, we tend to spend more time justifying ourselves than asking how God wants to move through us.

For others, it's a question of *calling*. The person might understand that their calling to the business world is no less than a person called to work at a church, but they still wonder how to live out their faith in their office. Is evangelism their main responsibility? Or is it giving financially to Christian ministry? Or using their expertise on a church finance committee? This approach eventually devolves into a comfortable complacency. The person identifies his or her contribution and faithfully attends to it, while the rest of life remains untouched.

Lastly, for others—perhaps most people—reconciling their career and their faith is not a question they've seriously considered. Simply attending church each week is sacrifice enough when life is filled with the struggle to pay off student loans, hit sales targets, and balance kids' sports with the demands of a career.

So, what does it mean to be a Christian businessperson?

I believe that is the wrong question. Our career is not our identity. Our calling, though important, is not our identity. Rather than obsessing over *what we do*, we must start by remembering *who we are*. The question we must ask is what does it mean to be a Christian? The answer to that question is found through a lifetime of discipleship, but it reveals a fundamental mistake in which we assume our career somehow changes our call to follow Jesus.

We live in the age of specialists. Doctors care for the body, teachers educate the young, pastors care for the soul, and businesspeople run the economy so we can all eat—or so we imagine. This way of thinking is not found in Scripture; instead, the Bible offers a radically different approach. Ministry is not the specialized function of the trained professional, nor is it the vocation of the priestly caste. All believers enter into ministry when they accept the call to follow Jesus. But we must be careful in how we define ministry. For the vast majority of believers, ministry will never involve a job at a church.

The last five verses in Matthew's Gospel are among the most famous in all of Scripture. This important biblical story occurs after the death, burial, and resurrection of Jesus. Through His blood, our identity has been eternally secured. We are adopted into God's family and we inherited His promise. Our career no longer defines us! We are defined by our life in God, and that frees us to understanding His purposes for our career. The Great Commission speaks right to the heart of our calling:

When the eleven disciples went to Galilee, to the mountain where Jesus had told them to go. When they saw him, they worshiped him; but some doubted. Then Jesus came to them and said, "All authority in heaven and on earth has been given to me. Therefore go and make disciples of all nations, baptizing

them in the name of the Father and of the Son and of the Holy
Spirit, and teaching them to obey everything I have command-
ed you. And surely I am with you always, to the very end of the
age." Matthew 28:16-20

Throughout Matthew, Jesus is revealed as the fulfillment of God's purposes for Israel. Matthew 1:1 shows that Jesus is in the lineage of both Abraham and David, which represents two major Old Testament themes of covenant and kingdom. In the Old Testament, God used Moses to lead Israel out of slavery. He then confirmed His covenant to Israel on Mount Sinai, taught them His ways, and established them as a nation—His chosen people. Jesus is a new Moses through whom God is teaching His ways, forming a new nation, and leading His people out of slavery and into the promise.

The whole Gospel builds to the Great Commission and beautifully ties the various themes of the book together. Jesus's ministry began on a mountain teaching His disciples, and then His earthly ministry ended on a mountain sending His disciples to teach others. Jesus once sent His disciples on a temporary mission throughout Israel, but after His resurrection, He sent His disciples on a permanent mission throughout all the nations. Prior to His death, Jesus warned His disciples about the end of the age, but prior to His ascension, He promised to be with them until the very end. His resurrection changed everything and frees us to walk in His purposes.

We inherited this commission to make disciples. Making disciples begins when we live as disciples. We must prioritize prayer because Jesus is the one with the authority. We share our faith because Jesus alone can save. We live counter-culturally in the way we treat people, money, and power because we are committed to obeying His commands.

To make disciples, we must live this way in community and invite others to join us. Like Brandon's story, this may start with two co-workers praying before work once a week. It may be as simple as praying for a few people every day and then looking for God opportunities to serve them and share your faith. Disciple-making is not a complicated process we must learn but rather a lifestyle we must commit to live.

Discipleship starts as we go. Many English translations render the command "go," but it is probably better written "as you are going." The mission of God rarely involves quitting your job to join the ministry; instead, it is embracing your ministry at your job. For some, God calls them to go to foreign nations or into new vocations, but all believers are called to a lifestyle of disciple-making wherever God has placed them.

ANOTHER IN THE FIRE

I used to think God would always save me from the furnace;
now I know, he wants to put another in the fire with me.

When people hear about the wonderous things God has done in our workplace, I am almost always asked one of two questions:

"How'd your business revival start?"

"What would you say are the key one or two things people could do to start a revival in their workplace?"

My answer is simple: pray and find yourself a Gary. The first response needs little or minimal explanation; however, the second requires some backstory.

It was nearly ten years ago now, but the aches and the pains of my first few years with my current employer still feel fresh. My wonderful wife and I left Fort Worth, Texas, to move closer to home, and I took an entry-level sales position with my current company. On paper, everything about our decision was crazy. I left a prominent role in the banking industry and turned down a promotion to move, while Kristin left her career completely. We dropped to one income, had zero community, and were learning to care for our newborn son. Moreover, the new sales role was extremely difficult to learn. The piece of the puzzle I thought would be the easiest, selling stuff, was one of the hardest. We felt God was calling us to go, so it should be easier, right?

During the first ninety days in my new role, ten salespeople were terminated for lack of performance or for ethical reasons. This may not seem like a large number to some, but the total number of sales positions was thirty-one. I couldn't discern a rhythm or a pattern to the terminations—tenure, team, leadership. Some of the fired employees were extremely successful in the past but just had one bad year or couple of quarters. To say I was stressed is the understatement of the century. (One income plus a new baby and then people getting canned all around equals a lot of stress!)

As I continued to work on my sales pipeline and my sleep patterns, with a newborn, stayed irregular, the weight of my new normal became increasingly heavy. I had a constant "looking over the shoulder" mentality. I watched men and women get fired who were successful at this role, while I had not sold a single thing yet. In all this uncertainty, I felt completely powerless in my stress. I could not unload the full weight of my pressure to Kristin because she was also struggling in the transition. I knew I needed something.

I remember walking into my office after eighty days in my role to see the Executive Vice President waiting for me with a yellow notepad at six o'clock in the morning. He was the one who had fired everyone.

"Good Morning," I quivered.

"Morning, let's make some calls," He firmly replied.

With perspiration breaking out on my forehead, I sat straight down in my chair, picked up my headset, and started making sales calls. After about an hour and a half, the Executive V.P. recapped what he had observed, and it was less than stellar. He stood up. He gave me a few more pointers and started to leave. As he walked out of my office he turned and gave me one phrase of wisdom:

"Brandon, willpower beats skill every time. Keep coming in and learning; your skill will improve, but your WILL to succeed is all on you."

As soon as he was out of sight, I closed my office door and pressed my head against the wall. Slightly out of sight from the window and standing in the corner, I began to talk to God. I could feel the emotion from a career change, new town, new baby, and lack of success welling up deep inside me.

"What am I doing here?" I mumbled.

That's when I heard the gentle reply from the still small voice inside my aching tired soul, "My WILL doesn't require skill or talent, just WILLINGNESS."

In that deep moment of questioning everything around me, I knew there was nothing inside of me that could have manufactured that phrase. There was a promise that pointed beyond my short comings. I could feel the stillness inside me silence all my fears. Though peace had momentarily poured over me like warm honey, I knew I still needed strength and courage to move to action. I knew God had sent me to this company. I knew he had sent me to this town. I simply needed him to send me back into my chair and onto the phone.

God gave me the strength to finish out my day and my week. However, like clockwork, on the following Monday the Executive Vice President was waiting for me again at six o'clock in the morning. I puffed out a "Good, morning" and reached immediately for the phone. For exactly one and half hours, he listened, critiqued, and wrote down more notes. Only this time, as he was leaving, he gave me exactly what I needed to hear for God to plant a seed in my soul.

"Brandon, you are getting better. You still have a long way to go to be good at this game, but if you keep after it, if you record and listen to your calls, and if you partner with someone to listen to them with you, then you will get it."

"Thank you, sir. Will you be here next Monday too?" I asked confidently.

"Not sure, how come?" He frowned.

"Well sir, good is the enemy of great. I want you to keep coming until I surpass good, because *good* won't get my family where *great* will."

With a quick smirk on his face, he nodded and closed my door behind him. My boss' boss had simultaneously unlocked something inside of me physically and spiritually. The prior week the fear he invoked pushed me into a corner to hear the voice of God telling me he brought me here. Then, the follow-up encounter called out the man of God inside me to push through to the physical. I had been so fearful of being fired that I stopped searching for ways to stay planted inside the will of God. I realized in that first six o'clock meeting that God sent me here to prosper and for his purpose. In the second meeting I realized when God sent me on a mission, he also sent the way to accomplish it. When Mr. Tunmire, my Executive V.P., told me to partner with someone for my physical success, he also imbedded a piece of God's promise deeper into my spiritual mission. I needed someone to partner with me spiritually. I needed a prayer partner.

As this thought ran through my mind, I quickly dismissed it. Prayer partner? We weren't even going to church in Waco yet. Isn't it amazing how some of our deepest and most meaningful revelations come from places of great desperation? God was up to something deeper. I pushed the idea of a prayer partner aside and started looking for a partner for my business success. Two days later, I walked into Gary Landon's office and asked him if he would help me develop the skill I was lacking. He agreed. Gary had been a successful salesperson in our company for five straight years and was always willing to help anyone who asked.

Over the next several weeks, I made calls and charged down the hallway to Gary's office for guidance. All the while, Mr. Tunmire continued to pop in every Monday at six o'clock sharp to listen to calls. One day, I marched into Gary's office and noticed him high fiving another team member. Gary had just closed two more sales. I had still closed zero. This is when the ridiculously competitive nature took over.

"How are you doing it? I can't seem to get one done and you are closing two at a time."

"Well, I have been doing this a little longer," Gary graciously tried to affirm me.

Not to be deterred, I pressed him further and asked if there was something I wasn't doing. In complete Gary fashion, he responded again with grace and humbleness, but then he challenged me.

"Brandon, you are doing a good job, but I have to give all the credit back to God for my success."

Click.

The door of God's plan had just unlocked inside my soul. I drilled down beyond what I deemed a normal "Christian" response and found something deeper. For the first time since I started my role, I put myself aside and asked Gary to tell me his story. I was amazed. What I had brushed off as common Christian lingo was deep faith and belief. The man I had been running to for help was daily running to the cross for his help. This was not his secret; it was his lifestyle.

"Would you be willing to start meeting and praying with me? Like maybe once a week in the morning?"

"Sure, I work out Monday, Wednesday, and Friday mornings. But how about Tuesday?" Gary replied.

"Tuesday is perfect. That's Mr. Tunmire's late day," I chuckled.

Unbeknownst to either of us, this simple conversation would be the catalyst to the move of God in our company. However, His ways are not our ways. Gary and I met that very next Tuesday to pray. Gary and I poured out our hearts to the throne of heaven and prayed for everything we could think of for thirty minutes. It was powerful. So much so, that he and I continued to meet every Tuesday. Our prayer meetings didn't flip some immediate switch to success or stop the termination rate; however, it kept us focused on what was important. Gary and I sent emails and personal invites to other colleagues to join us to no avail. We pressed inward. I kept showing up early to sharpen my skills in the sales role and did everything I could to be an employee of excellence. We kept praying.

In the next eighteen months, the termination rate for sales professionals in our role reached three-hundred and fifty percent. Mr. Tunmire continued to listen to my calls on Monday mornings. I was named rookie of the year. Gary and I became number one and number two in production for our team. But we did not add to our prayer circle, despite numerous pleas and attempts. We continued anyway. There were multiple times when a "joking" salesperson mocked us for our Tuesday prayer. We always quickly responded, "You are welcome to join us anytime."

There is not one single doubt in my mind that my skill would have improved over the same time period due to the amount of work I put into it even if I had not prayed. But there is also not one doubt that my *will* would have been broken completely. I watched over one hundred talented sales professionals be terminated during that eighteen-month timeframe. I needed that simple prayer meeting to keep me centered on God bringing me to this company. I had another man to lean on and to lift when needed. I looked forward to those Tuesdays...and still do.

When I asked Gary to pray with me, Kristin and I were not even going to church. We had a newborn, and I didn't have much of a devotional life to speak of. I knew Jesus, but He had not become a part of my everyday life until that Tuesday prayer meeting. The Lord brought me a man in Gary Landon who was faithful and fruitful. He had the success in sales I wanted, but it wasn't until I heard him pray that I realized he had way more that I wanted. Before the business revival could take place in our company it had to take place inside of *me*.

I realized through those meetings that *God wouldn't move mightily through me until He had moved greatly inside me*. It was during this prayer time with Gary that I started to see what I had witnessed with Bill so many years earlier. My job is not just about closing sales or hitting targets; it is a journey of walking with Jesus every day. This requires a reorientation, a new way of viewing the workplace, and this is the first step toward a business revival.

"Let us not become weary in doing good, for at the proper time we will reap a harvest if we do not give up." Galatians 6:9

✳

No matter where you are in your career or your company, ask God to bring to you a Gary. I am still not sure what gave me the courage to ask Gary to pray with me; it could have been fear, it could have been something else. However, he has been a faithful prayer warrior with me for almost a decade straight. There have been many ups and downs along the way but having a faithful prayer partner has been a necessity. On multiple occasions, Gary and I rushed into our Tuesday Morning prayer gasping, "I need it today, brother."

If you want to bring change to your company, city, state, and beyond, know that it starts with one, then another, and then another. Ask God to change you first, and then ask him to bring another to come alongside you. What God started in that one-on-one prayer with Gary has become much greater than we could have imagined. We have seen salvations, miraculous healings, countless people set free from bondage, and many families restored. All from two men faithfully running to the throne of the King.

If you want to start a revival in your workplace then start by praying for one. Ask God to send you one more person to pray with, and another, and another.

✳

"As iron sharpens iron, so one person sharpens another." Proverbs 27:17

Chapter 3

PRAY. NOW

I used to think when people wanted me to pray for them that later was okay. Now I am aware that later seldom happens.

"Brother, I need to tell you what God has been pressing on me."

It was a Tuesday morning prayer time with my friend Gary, a Tuesday like many Tuesdays before, but this time something was different. I could feel his intensity dripping from every pore. Gary's eyes stayed locked with mine.

"Sure, what's up?" I engaged.

Up until this point, Gary and I had been praying for almost eighteen months with little momentum. He and I had invited anyone and everyone we could, but it was usually just us. We asked every Christian we came across if they wanted to pray with us, but we mostly just received excuses and reasons why they could not join.

"I was reading in Luke 11, and now get this!" Gary reached his palm towards my chest.

With a few swift motions, Gary began to scroll his tablet to the chapter he had referenced. As the passion charged from deep inside my friend, he quickly read the verse out loud:

"One day Jesus was praying in a certain place. When he finished,

one of his disciples said to Him, 'Lord, teach us to pray, just as John taught his disciple.'" Luke 11: 1 (NIV)

"Brandon, God is calling us to PRAY!" Gary's eyes flickered like an insane man.

"Amen, Bro. That's what we are here for." I grinned.

"No, you don't get it!" he quickly charged back.

It did not take a rocket scientist to figure out Gary and I were on different pages. The same book, just different pages. I knew what Gary was saying, because I had heard the same verbiage a thousand times. That was the problem.

"Let's read that verse again. Remember, the disciples had spent tons of time with Jesus. They could have asked him to teach them how to do healings, preach better, or perform any one of a dozen miracles, but they said, 'Teach us to Pray.' Why is that? Because they recognized they were not doing what Jesus was doing. Brandon, these guys were Jews, they were 'brought up in church,' they knew HOW to pray...but they didn't," Gary's passion echoed.

In a moment of pure honesty, I replied, "So, what do we do?"

I had read the scripture Gary had referenced before, but the passion and the fresh look at the words intrigued me. I knew what my friend had just said was a powerful revelation in the making. If I was a disciple, Gary was right, I would have asked Jesus to teach me to do the "cool stuff." Unless...

"How many times do we get asked to pray for people?" Gary's tone became softer.

"All the time."

"Exactly, all the time. But how often do we say, 'Yeah sure,' and forget?" His eyes glimmered.

"All the time." I shook my head.

"I want to change that!" Gary charged forward.

In this moment of powerful simplicity, Gary and I quickly made a covenant with one another. We told each other we would keep one another accountable to *Pray Now* if someone asked. If anyone came to us, asking for prayer, we committed to drop whatever we were doing and pray. We stretched out our palms and even shook on it. Then, as we sat in my worn-out office chairs to pray, a face peaked through the window. It was Nathan, a newer salesperson in our department. I smiled and waved him inside.

"Hey, guys. I have a call to make, but do you think you could pray for me today? I mean, it's no secret I am struggling in sales, and it's...I mean...you guys get it, this is the hardest job I have ever had. But I need this job, and I think I might be on the chopping block." Nathan grimaced.

As he stood, completely non-committal, Gary and I smiled at one another.

"Step on inside." I stood up promptly.

"Well, I have a call and..."

"When's your call?" Gary popped back.

"Like soon, in five minutes." Nathan grabbed his watch.

"Oh, perfect. This will only take two." Gary stood.

In a swift instant, Gary and I poured prayer over our friend and sent him to make his call on time. However, before he left Gary and I both offered to help him learn verbiage and tools we had used to be successful. We told him when he was done with his morning calls, or if it needed to be another day, we would gladly pass on any knowledge we could. We did not just pray and wish him the best. We offered to "walk alongside him" and told him we would follow up. Nathan thanked us through watery eyes and looked down at his watch. "Three minutes to spare." A gentle chuckle shot through my office as he left.

"Do you see what I mean?!" Gary's palm smacked my arm in excitement.

"You can't make this stuff up." I grinned.

It was exactly as if God heard what we had promised and said, "Great, boys. Here you go." In that sweet Tuesday morning moment, God had gently nudged Gary and me out of the stands and into the actual arena. We had been praying for people, but not actually praying for people. For almost eighteen months straight, Gary and I had met weekly and begged God for a revival. But we did not see revival until we were willing to get serious about asking Jesus how to pray and then step outside of cultural norms to do so.

As Christians we consistently tell people we will pray for them and then forget. I know countless times I have asked people to pray for me and watched them smile and walk away without petitioning the throne of God. "Pray for me" or "I'll pray for you" has become as common to believers as "Good Morning" or "Bless you" after a sneeze. We need the same posture as the disciples: Lord teach us to pray!

*

I have never seen a time when we would have so much national division, and our division has put us in a defensive position. As a result, we look at everyone and everything as a possible threat to our happiness. Even Christians are leery of other Christians more now than ever before. Therefore, instead of reaching out to one another, we hold it inside. We confidently go "through the motions" and know the verbiage, but we won't pour out our fears and burdens to one another.

We hold each other at arm's length, test the waters with common redundancy and move on. This attitude must shift. If you receive nothing else from this book, hear this: a business revival will take place with this one simple change in your mentality. When someone asks you to pray for them, PRAY RIGHT THERE.

*

A major shift took place for Gary and me after we prayed for Nathan. Not right away. Not even in the next month. However, after a few weeks of us praying on the spot and following up to help Nathan with his sales learning, a shift happened. Nathan got his first sale and confidently proclaimed (without prompting) his path changed after a Tuesday prayer meeting. Two months later, Gary and I slowly had more knocks on our door for prayer. The movement had begun with consistency, boldness, brothers in arms, and a spontaneous two-minute prayer. The movement has also taken hold in another company as well. Nathan was later recruited by another sales organization where he now holds prayer meetings on Tuesday mornings.

"if my people, who are called by my name, will humble themselves and pray and seek my face and turn from their wicked ways, then I will hear from heaven, and I will forgive their sins and will heal their land." 2 Chronicles 7:14

*

Today, one of my greatest joys is being in a room and hearing a knock on the door, followed by a simple, "Can you pray for...?" I love to walk up and down the hallway and see sales professionals clutched in prayer. It's a joy to walk by an office and hear someone shout, "Hey, B! Pop in here. Someone just asked for prayer." The shift in our culture that day with Gary has sparked a fire inside the team to become prayer warriors. We have other people from different departments who come to the sales building *for prayer*. We have had prayer "pop-ins" for everything under the sun. The most common for us are: Healing (sickness), Infertility, and Salvation. I don't think it is a coincidence that when you form an acronym with the big three you get H.I.S. Because when you surrender your life to loving God and loving people, you have no choice but to become HIS in the place he has you.

Through the simple action of praying for people when they ask, the pillars in our workplace have seen almost one hundred salvations, countless healings, and God stir hope in men and woman who were hopeless. In addition to Nathan, I have ten former employees who have left or been hired away and have started their own prayer meetings based on this one practice. Many of these amazing folks still come back to our prayer group from time to time. Instead of seeing employees as "a means" to a better budget or a personal gain, I see them as potential highly skilled missionaries to grow or send. This one simple tool, Pray NOW, is the catalyst for change. It is also the easiest. When someone asks you to pray for them, pray right there! See what God can do through you!

Chapter 4

OFFICE CHAIR SALVATION

I used to think I had to be overly prepared for God to move.
Now I know I just need to be PRESENT.

I still remember my first workplace salvation conversation. It
had been a long week of training new owners and entertaining new
guests. It was finally Friday, and I had been working twelve days
straight. I shut down my computer and grabbed my keys. A new franchise owner and his manager needed a ride back to their hotel, so I
shut down a few minutes early to pick them up. He and I had become
close friends during the yearlong process of him becoming a new
owner.

(Knock, Knock)

"I was literally just closing my computer to come get you guys.
Did y'all finish early?" I asked my friend.

"Nah, I just needed a break. I've been walking down by the park
and now here." He shrugged.

My friend was normally a joyful jokester, but today he looked
downcast. As he gently eased into one of my fake leather chairs, I
asked him if he was okay. With a quick shake, my three-hundred-
pound comrade folded his head into his hands. The gentle giant was

at an emotional breaking point.

"Talk to me, buddy." I wrapped my arm around his shoulder.

"I don't know what to do." Tears filled his eyes.

Even though all I wanted was to end my day and head home, I allowed my plans to be interrupted, and I simply sat to listen to the heartache choking my friend. I was present. He quickly explained that his marriage was in shambles and his business was falling apart at the seams. With each gentle sob from this mighty man, he walked me through the life he had been trying to keep a secret. My friend had been putting on a "happy face" for everyone around: his family, his employees, his church, and his friends. He thought this façade would make life better and masked the deep need for truth and healing. The aching man crying beside me was imprisoned by the very thing he thought would free him. He was a pastor of a small church in New England. This business was the side hustle for paying his mortgage.

"I am so sorry, buddy. How can I help?" I leaned closer to comfort him.

"I'm not sure anyone can." He paused to wipe snot from his face. "I don't even know why I am telling you this stuff; I haven't told anyone."

"I am glad you trust me. What else is going on? Is there more?" I smiled.

As this mountain of a man slumped backward in my chair, the leather creaked loudly under his weight. With a massive exhale, his eyes stayed fixed on the floor under his black work boots. The silence over the next several minutes created almost a preverbal game of chicken—who would speak first? He did and I won the game no one knew we were playing.

"I mean, I know the answers, B. I know I just need faith like a mustard seed. I am a pastor, right?" He paused to exhale loudly. "But I mean, I need God to move my mountains. I believe he can. But he won't for some reason."

As my friend shifted back and forth in his chair, I simply listened to him. I didn't rush into his pain and tell him, "Oh, I know…" or "I understand." I just listened. As his tears flowed, I put my agenda aside for as long as he needed. My role in his moment of hurting was to bring comfort, not advice. Many Christians believe we must have all the answers in these moments. Instead, a simple, "I am so sorry" has more power. I am not his Holy Spirit or his inner healer. However, I can be a friend who loves and leads by listening. His emotions started to calm, and he thanked me for just listening. I wrapped my arms around him.

"Brother, can I pray for you?" I smiled.

He agreed. I put my right arm around his massive shoulders and prayed over every area of his life. It was a normal moment of prayer, but what happened next could only be God. A question popped into my mind that I had never asked my friend. This is where everything changed. We both stood, as if to walk out, and I walked over to my desk for my keys. I must have laid them down when he entered.

"How did you come to know Jesus?" I reached for the keys not even looking at my friend.

"I mean, I grew up in a Christian home, so I have always been a Christian."

"Right, I remember you saying that before, but when did it become your faith? Like, at what age?" I responded.

My friend quickly recounted every Sunday growing up, his seminary studies, and everything he "knew" about Jesus. He even seasoned the conversation, like a fine steak, with scriptures peppered throughout his memories. It was masterful. It was well rehearsed. It was not what I asked. As I listened to all his "churchy" answers, we stayed standing in the doorway of my office.

"Right, but when did you surrender your life to Jesus?" I spoke more plainly.

"I just told you." He seemed frustrated as he frowned.

I didn't want to insult him or just keep asking the same questions over and over, so I paused and asked him a different question. (I secretly think Jesus loves salespeople a little bit more.)

"When you preach and do an altar call and people come forward, what do you do when they get there?" I replied.

With a quick huff, my friend went through the steps of the sinner's prayer, frowned, talked about people coming forward, and even quoted Romans 10:9 to me.

"If you declare with your mouth, "Jesus is Lord," and believe in your heart that God raised him from the dead, you will be saved."
Romans 10:9 (NIV)

"When did YOU do that?" I pointed at him.

The look of frustration on the face in front of me turned softer. His eyes shifted away from mine. I stayed silent as I watched his mind searching his memory bank. His shoulders dropped. He shoved his hands quickly into his pockets and rocked gently. It was as if the question had caused paralyses to his tongue. While he shifted gently back and forth, I tucked my keys neatly into my dress slacks and crossed my arms. Intently, I kept my eyes locked on the man, a foot taller than me, swaying nervously from side to side. A minute felt like ten minutes. My friend who always had something to say mumbled a little phrase I couldn't hear, then his eyes began to water.

"I don't know that I ever did," he shrugged.

"That you ever did what?" I asked with vigor.

"I can't remember ever saying the prayer for myself. I can't remember anyone even asking me. I don't think I...no...I know I haven't ever said it."

As his silence changed into a rapid fire of ramblings, I gently smiled into his uncertainty and stood patiently in front of my pastor friend. He quickly tried to rationalize his position and even said, "I mean, I have prayed the prayer hundreds of times with other people, so I mean, I have prayed it, right?"

"Do you want to know for certain? I mean, really know? We can do it right here." I uncrossed my arms and pointed to my dirty green office carpet.

As if someone had pushed him, he fell back into my fake leather chair. My friend quickly leaned forward and clutched his hands together.

"Yes, let's do it!" he said emphatically.

I plopped myself down beside him. Once I leaned in next to my friend, he unclasped his hands and wrapped his arm around my shoulders. As he pulled me in tightly, he repeated after me, "Lord, I am a sinner. I know you sent your son Jesus to die for me, and that he was raised from the dead for me. Forgive me of my sins and come and be my savior forever."

Immediately, when we finished praying, my friend wrapped both arms around me and thanked me for the courage I had to ask.

That day God did something massive for both my friend and me. He showed me that we don't have to be theologians or pastors to be used by God—we just must be present and willing. The fire of a movement inside our place of work started with a pastor coming to know Jesus! As of today, many people have come to know Jesus as their Savior inside our workplace, and it started with a pastor. Jesus can start wherever he wants, but for me, He had to start here. He had to show me not to guess or judge who needs Jesus, but to let Him do that. I just need to ask the question and the question behind the question. I am not the Holy Spirit. I am not the way, the truth, or the life...He is.

This chapter is not a battle of theology, nor is it meant to engage centuries-old debates about the timing and nature of salvation. Instead, this is a story about a real person encountering a real God. My friend and I had a relationship that allowed me to ask the questions I did. Do we know the salvation story of my friend completely? No.

However, he will tell you that that day in my office was the day that he said "yes" to Jesus and everything changed. After he went home, we spoke almost daily, and the conversations were completely different. He would tell you, as he told me, that the Scriptures came alive after that day. His marriage was different. His joy was real and not manufactured. My role was to respond to the prompting inside my spirit and be willing to ask the question. There was no secret sauce or theological trickery. It was friends sitting down in an office and having a real conversation about things that matter.

Today this man of God is still running his business and pastoring his church. However, since that day in the office, his church size has tripled, and his business is spread across three New England states. He employs forty people, and I have led Bible studies with them via webinars (before work). Every time my friend introduces me, he says, "Dis is the brotha who cared enough about me to bring me Jesus for real, not just a prayer—a new life."

Are you willing to ask the hard questions, even to people you think have the answer already? Are you willing to pray? Are you willing to just love people? That is all a revival needs, a willing friend.

Chapter 5

CIRCLE MAKING

I used to think I was a square peg in a round hole.
Now I know I was made to make circles.

In 2014, a client of mine gave me a book that radically changed my spiritual trajectory. The previous year I had been promoted for the first time, and I was still in a team transition period. This client was from the Washington D.C. area, and his family were members of National Community Church there. He handed me the book and said, "Careful with this, it will rock your world." Following his strict "You need to read this" and persistent follow-up over the next several months, I did like all Christian believers I knew—I put it on the shelf and forgot about it. I even started to avoid his phone calls. But God had planted a seed inside my bookshelf, office, and heart.

I kept the book perfectly nestled between my ceramic bull bookend and other business titles for almost a full year. As God would have it, I was promoted a second time in January 2015, and asked to move to the corner office. While I was packing books to be transferred, one of my team members came to help.

"The Circle Maker?" Oh, Mark Batterson, he's good. Have you read more of his stuff? My wife and I really like his preaching, and he

has such a great delivery." He held the book up towards me.

"Nah, a client gave that to me last year. Haven't had a chance to read it. Do you want to read it?" I shrugged back.

"Haven't had a chance? Brandon, you read like crazy. You mean you just don't want to read it, probably because the client told you that you have to read it! That's my guess." He laughed.

"What's that supposed to mean?"

"It means, anyone who knows you, at ALL, knows telling you that you have to do something means it ain't happening. He should have said, 'Brandon, I bet you can't read this book in a week.'"

Even though I tried to rebut him and pleaded for him to just grab the books and help me pack, I knew he was right.

My entire life, I have wanted to conquer the impossible—promote me to the worst team in the company, give me the brand no one can sell—I want the road less traveled. I want "can't win" situations, because they become "can't lose" moments. My friend did exactly what I needed.

"I bet you can't read that book by next Friday. I will bet you lunch!"

As he stuck out his hand to shake on it, I raised the ante. "How about lunch, plus twenty dollars if YOU can read it faster."

Ridiculous. Once we shook on the final wager, we both laughed at the life of competitive sales professionals, and he jokingly asked if he could still borrow the book for the week. *No. Good luck though.* At least he helped me pack the rest of my books. When the book boxes and the rest of my stuff landed into my new office, I finally cracked open the book.

Within a few short pages, I was intrigued far beyond the twenty-dollar lunch victory. The simple stories and foundation of *The Circle Maker* grabbed something deep inside my soul. That weekend, my wife and I took a short getaway and I devoured the book. The stories of prayer caused me to reflect deeply. What am I contending for at this moment? Am I "drawing circles" around my biggest challenges? My family? All weekend long, I relaxed by the lake and journaled my thoughts and personal revelations. I knew the act of drawing a circle didn't have to be a physical one, yet God was calling me to petition his throne with my praises and prayer. I understood that, for the first time, God wanted to be a part of my successes as much as he wanted me to beg for his help in my failures. There was an atmospheric shift deep inside my soul.

Without truly knowing it, I had come to the end of myself. In one book. In one weekend. This new revelation hit me like a ton of bricks. I was completely willing to run to God with my regrets and mistakes, but I wanted the credit for all my successes. I had just been given increased management responsibilities and I needed help. I knew what made me successful with a small team would not help me with the new, doubled in size team. I was reading the book on a bet, but my need gave it a place to marinate.

I returned to work Monday, victorious, with a new purpose. When my friend and team member made it to the office, I marched in excitedly.

"Did you read the book?" I grinned.

"You didn't finish!" he replied.

"I did. But did you?"

"Yeah, I got some of it. It's a good story so far." He started to settle in for the day.

"It was powerful. Now I am stuck trying to decide how to apply what I learned."

"How about you just start?" He shrugged.

"Great idea. Where's my money?" I poked back.

Even though my friend was half-joking, his sarcastic jab had struck a nerve—in a good way. He was right. I had taken a revelation about prayer and trapped it inside my own religious understanding. I did what I had always done: wait for "confirmation" to move. Yet today, something was different. When my lunch hour arrived, I still didn't know where or who to start praying over, so I marched outside.

I started walking around the building and prayed. On about the third lap, I looked back toward the building and noticed people staring back through the windows. Had one of their leaders gone a little crazy? Had Brandon finally had enough? After I walked back inside, several people asked, "What were you doing?"

"Just praying. Needed it today."

For the next two months, Monday through Friday, I walked around the building praying over my teams. I prayed for the success of the entire team and organization. I must have quoted Psalm 5:12 hundreds of times:

"Surely, LORD, you bless the righteous; you surround them with favor as with a shield."

I felt foolish almost every time I started my prayer walks. However, as I continued to place one foot in front of the other, my strength began to build. The mockers and gawkers eventually stopped staring out their windows, but I kept marching. My team's sales cratered. I kept marching. My star salesman sold zero for six months. My father was diagnosed with cancer a second time. I was forced to pay tens of thousands of dollars in taxes because of a mistake. I kept circling. If it was cold outside I still prayer walked. Rainy? I got soaked. I am not a quitter. I am bull-headed and stubborn as the day is long. God called me to prayer walk so that is what I did, but life grew more difficult in the process. Why? I asked God this question repeatedly.

My answer came in the form of another leader in our company. It was raining slightly when I zipped up my coat to head outside. He popped out of his office by the back door.

"Still going strong, huh?" he snickered.

"Yep." I held the door open.

"How long you gonna keep this up?" He chuckled.

"As long as it takes."

As I pulled up the hood to my raincoat, I felt the frustration welling up behind my eyes. I walked the first lap around in complete silence. No praying. No speaking. Just steps. Then the second lap around I passed my counterpart smiling. He was tucked under the overhang with a few other people. The grins and jabs came bellowing forward. I lovingly jabbed back and kept marching.

"Lord, what am I doing?" I mumbled to myself.

I felt a still small voice inside the pit of my stomach answer back: "You are walking in circles."

"I am trying to give my family, my business, my finances, my teams, and my prayers over to you," I muttered.

Again, a thought entered my mind, "No, you are trying desperately to control every area of your life and be seen walking in circles. Is this for me or you?"

I stopped. I lifted my face towards the gray sky. With cold rain dancing across my beard and glasses, I simply asked God to take it all. Then I did something that had not crossed my mind: I asked God to walk with me. It was the most refreshing time I had walking in six months. I finally transitioned from going on a prayer walk to walking with my Heavenly Father. I had been asking God to lift my load, heal my father, provide financially, and help my teams like a spoiled child. Even though I knew I was walking for Him, I had not walked with him.

It's wise to choose your battles when you can, but what will you do when your battle chooses you? I had made a religion of walking around our building. Instead of asking God, "How should I circle today? Do I go into the offices of my team members and pray for them? Walk prayer circles around my parent's house? Walk inside the building or outside? Write names on a piece of paper and circle it with red ink each time I pray for them?" I needed a new battle plan. I needed my Papa-God to carry me through the steps.

I had been telling anyone who would listen that the battle was God's, but I lived in the stress of believing that success rested on me. I started marching out of fear of stopping. God gently reminded me the purpose of prayer is Him. That rainy-day mockery led to a powerful discovery. I am absolutely made to fight battles in prayer. And I am made to do it with God.

I started asking God each day, "How should we circle today?" Somedays it was crystal clear while on other days, a team member popped in my mind or knocked at the door. There are still days when I simply walk around the inside of the building and gently tap on doors as I go by and ask God to bless each person.

Once I started asking, "Lord, teach me to pray today," everything shifted. The unmovable mountains started to move. I discovered that faith must be in a Person, not an outcome. When I made this shift, it gave me confidence whether I saw the external breakthrough or not. In the process I learned one of the most valuable lessons—God wants His battle back. The battles I was facing kept growing because I was trying to fight them with my strength, not His. My prayers shifted from, "Take this away, Lord" to "What do we do with this Papa?"

When this revelation of prayer became reality in my spirit, we broke every record in our company's three decades of sales history. My friend Gary and I saw our prayer group grow. We saw people come to know Jesus in our offices. We saw our first healing. But more than all this, my teams and their families got to witness the power of walking in prayer with our God. By the end of 2015, other team members started circling the building in prayer, Monday through Friday. Today, we still circle our building in prayer. We just ask God how first.

"...Lord, teach us to pray..." Luke 11:1

PASTORAL PERSPECTIVE: THE BODY OF CHRIST

We live in a highly individualistic and consumeristic culture. Most of us view life through the lens of *self*. *I* am the center of *my* world. *I* care about *my* career, *my* income, and *my* retirement. And it quickly gets spiritualized as we focus on *my* calling and *my* spiritual gifts. In this self-centered way of thinking, my career is primarily focused on me, the church is reduced to a consumer good, and my calling is just another step toward my own sense of self-fulfillment.

Scripture teaches us an entirely different way of viewing the world. According to the teaching of Jesus, we find life when we realize life is not about us. Those who seek to save their lives will lose them, but those who lose their lives for His sake will find them. Business revival is not a matter of evangelistic technique—it is a heart change and an invitation into the life of a disciple.

If I am a disciple of Jesus, then I am a member of His Body. Have you ever taken time to reflect on this common metaphor? Throughout the New Testament, one of the main illustrations used to describe the Church is Christ's Body. This metaphor is powerful and holds profound implications if we take it seriously.

Jesus is the Head of His Body. My job is not to change the world or start a revival—that's Jesus's job. My job is to follow the leadership of the Head. Period. This understanding takes the pressure off us. Jesus working through His Body will establish His kingdom on the earth. We have the incredible privilege of partnering in His work, but He alone is in the driver's seat. It's like a child doing yard work with his father—He doesn't need our help but chooses us all the same.

A Body is more than the sum of its individual parts. The parts each matter but they find their fullness only when they are connected to the whole. A disconnect finger just isn't that helpful. Being the Body means that we find our identity in Jesus *together*, and it is through this revelation that we discover our own calling and are sent back out into the world to be his witness.

Participating in Christ's Body is so much more than attending a church service once per week. Don't get me wrong, Sunday worship and small group discipleship are fundamentally important. The problem is that we fail to recognize God's leadership the rest of the week. We need to gather together as God's people, but this gathering must then commission us to holistically live as the Body of Christ all throughout our city.

Every time you show up to your office, your classroom, or your clinic, you represent the hands and feet of Jesus to each person you interact with. This is an awesome responsibility and privilege. We do not engage God's mission alone—we are filled with His Spirit leading us and united together with fellow believers.

The Holy Spirit is working through each one of us everywhere we go. In the ancient world, a person's breath was synonymous with their spirit and was considered to be the animating lifeforce of their body. This is what the Holy Spirit does in Christ's Body. He is actively leading and uniting each member, empowering us to follow the leadership of Jesus.

Through the Spirit, God has placed you in community with others. You need believers who challenge, support, and encourage you. Sometimes you will personally see the fruit of revival, while at other times, you'll wonder if you are bearing any fruit at all, but you will never be alone.

A right understanding of the Body, with Christ as the Head and His Spirit bringing the life, frees us to fulfill our calling. Let's learn what it means to follow Jesus in the totality of our lives, including our career.

Chapter 6

FIGHT CLUB
BEAUTY AND BETRAYAL.

I used to think brothers in arms would consistently take a bullet for one another; Now I am aware, sometimes they are the ones behind the trigger.

The rain gently tapped against the pavement below my feet as I swiftly made my way across the parking lot. The gentle mist forced me to press my jacket tightly to my chest. Once I reached the building, I confidently made my way to our Human Resources department.

"Hey, Brandon. Come on in...." My HR director welcomed me.

With a quick glide, I removed my coat and closed the door behind me.

"Thanks for coming over to see us." My general council nodded.

I had partnered with our human resources department multiple times in my leadership, so the call to "pop over" and chat was not unordinary. However, a quick scan of their two faces revealed a difference.

"Cold out there, huh? Still raining?" My HR director nervously smiled.

"You know, my dad used to tell me that when people start talking about the weather, you better check for your wallet, so what's up?" I chuckled.

"Well, there has been a complaint that we need to bring to your attention," the attorney spoke up.

"Okay, lay it on me."

At this point, I still had no clue the conversation was about to take a turn. In complete honesty, working with driven, high performing, and overbearing sales professionals' complaints is simply a hazard of the business. I have been called to HR and forced to terminate or discipline employees for just about every complaint possible. If there were badges for this sort of thing, I would be an eagle scout. Nonetheless, my two colleagues shifted in their seats very professionally and responded.

"The complaint is about you."

"Me? For what?" I frowned.

Even as shock ran through me, I could feel a calm gently glide over my body. I knew in that moment I had not done anything wrong. The little southern boy inside me who had been conditioned to "just tell the truth" eagerly awaited my charges.

"Well, one of your 'guys' came to Human Resources and said that you have mandatory prayer meetings in your office."

"Which guy complained?" I retorted.

"You know we can't tell you that," my HR director quickly responded.

"But it's a guy?" I grinned.

"Can't tell you that either."

"Had to try. Was anything else said? Or just that? Because that is false," I replied calmly.

As the mixture of emotions crashed like waves inside my chest, I stayed calm and listened for their responses.

"Also, someone brought us this. Can you explain this one?" My attorney slid a golden coin towards me.

"The same guy? Or a different guy?"

"Well, we aren't saying it was a guy, but it's two individuals," my HR director rebutted.

I grabbed the coin from her desk and flipped it back and forth. On one side of the coin was a picture of a knight in armor with the words "Fight Club," and on the other side in blue letters: *Two rules 1) pray for everything 2) praise for everything.*

"Rejoice always, pray continually, give thanks in all circumstances; For this is God's will for you in Christ Jesus." I Thess 5:16-18.

I smiled gently at the verse on the coin while grappling with the overwhelming sense of hurt that smashed against my soul before I carefully replied.

"Well, one of the guys that has come into my office during the time on Fridays when I pray had these coins made." I pushed the coin back across the desk.

"So you didn't have these made to symbolize a prayer group or prayer club that happens in your office, and you didn't hand these out?" the corporate attorney quickly asked.

"Nope."

I could visibly see him mentally reformulating his questioning sequence. My uncomfortable silence and direct gaze didn't lend my two colleagues any favors. This is actually one of the most fundamental sales techniques I teach my teams. The mute button is your friend. We train diligently on answering the question that was asked, and then stop talking. I tell my teams consistently, "Are you still there?" or "Did I lose you?" is exactly what you want to hear in phone sales. My attorney friend paused and asked, "Anything else you want to add?" I had to smile, "No, just listening." Then almost right on que, that still small voice inside me brought a question into my mind.

"Are you guys saying that I can't pray in my office?" I frowned.

"Well, no. Of course not," my human resources director instantly replied.

"Oh, good. Because that would be a whole different Constitutional conversation, huh?" I grinned and winked.

I had partnered with these two many times, so I had the relationship deposits built up to be a little bolder. I understood fully that my corporate friends had a job to do, and I realized the deep implications of our conversation. Also, I would have completely agreed with their concerns if I had been "forcing" prayer, but I hadn't.

"Brandon, we are not saying you can't pray. You know my background, and my beliefs. We are aligned in our faith. But there has been a complaint, and we have to follow up on it. You are pretty bold with your faith, so if it makes someone uncomfortable enough to bring it to us then we need to follow up, right?" my corporate attorney added quickly.

"Are you asking me a question?" I replied.

With the truth dripping over our conversation, my colleagues offered more questions and I replied directly. The tone of my answers didn't change—honest, direct, non-defensive, even when I was asked, "Tell us what happens in these prayer meetings on Fridays." Every single bone in my body wanted to become a smart mouth! "Oh, we handle snakes, chant in robes, and drink Kool-Aid." However, I refrained from my sarcastic nature and told them how "I" prayed. In that, I could see the understanding and slight ease in their demeaner as we wrapped up our conversation.

"Brandon, you are a leader in this company. Also, we know in the sales building, you have some folks who are not as mature in these scenarios. We don't want guys using this as a manipulative sales tactic, and we will keep a close eye on this moving forward, just so you know," my attorney stated and pointed to his counterpart.

"Yeah, we just need you to be mindful and careful with what you communicate during your prayer time. We would, of course, recommend at the least that you make it well known it is optional and clearly that it is 'your prayer time' to protect you and the company," my HR director eloquently closed our meeting.

I rose from my chair and stuck out my hand. "Thank you both. I will absolutely be mindful as I pray in my office on Fridays at 8 o'clock, which is totally optional if you guys happen to stop by."

I grinned as my attorney friend swiftly told me to get out and repeated, "This is serious." I winked and apologized. Then I quickly responded, "I know it is. Thanks again, guys. Can I have this coin?"

Once I reached the parking lot and exhaled into the continuing mist, I started my conversation with my heavenly Papa. I quickly asked God for wisdom and searched my heart for bitterness. I recognized that bitterness would fester and hinder all God had started. I remembered the old adage that holding onto bitterness is like drinking poison and hoping the other person dies. I also recognized my corporate partners were right, and I needed to be careful. I felt betrayed in how it happened but also acknowledged the wisdom behind HR's concern.

None of this made the pain disappear. I later realized that there were only twenty-five coins made, which meant my accuser was someone close to me. I may never know their reasons; perhaps they were angry at one of my decisions or maybe it was an attempt to take my job. This moment reminded me of something Bill Pedigo taught me years ago, "Brandon, Christians will hurt you and cut you much deeper than the secular world ever could but love them anyway."

That Friday, five minutes before 8 o'clock, as my office began to fill with more and more guests, I silently watched each person enter. Not one thing was out of the ordinary—except my own heart. I had been fasting and praying for two days to release my bitterness and anger. Yet, in the moment of truth my flesh was clawing at my heart ravenously. I looked around the room and told them I would be right back. I strolled quickly into the bathroom and closed the stall door.

"Jesus, I need you. I am begging you to take this hurt, frustration, bitterness, and anger from my heart," I whispered.

In that moment, I was reminded of the betrayal Jesus had endured. Not in a churchy vacation Bible study way, but in a real way. One of his "brothers" betrayed him to his death – a man who walked with him, lived alongside him, and was "open" with him. Therefore, I changed my prayer.

"Jesus, break my heart for the walking wounded in this building and in this company, because to risk anything for you is an honor, Jesus. What can mere men do to me? Teach me to love anyway."

I marched back into my full office and smiled a "good morning." As I looked into the smiling faces, I closed the door and made my way back towards my desk.

"Good morning, y'all. Okay, before I pray, I want to make sure you all know this is optional and this is just me praying in MY office on a Friday. This is not mandatory. This is not something that you have to come to for this company or your job. Therefore, should any of you not want to be here or participate with ME praying in my office, you don't have to."

The ten faces around my cramped office stared back. As some frowned and few chuckled and glanced back and forth at one another, I closed my eyes and began to pray. With slight emotion in my voice, I prayed, thanked God, and then began to personalize a scripture back to heaven.

"Jesus, I thank you that I consider everything I have a loss because of the surpassing worth of knowing you. It's all garbage compared to you. If you have to, take it all, it's yours." Emotion gripped me tighter as I paused and continued, "I want to be found by you and you alone Lord. Jesus, teach me to rejoice always and to pray continually. I want to give thanks in ALL circumstances. Bless the men and woman in this building and this company. Surround them with blessing as a shield, even those who hate me or despise me, even those who wish to bring harm to my family, bless their socks off JE-SUS!" (Philippians 3:8-10, 1Thessalonians 5:16-18, Psalms 5:12).

I cannot remember the rest of my prayer that day; however, as I concluded I kept my eyes closed and sat gently back into my chair. Then one by one, without prompting, I could hear the emotion-filled prayers filling my office. There were confessions of bitterness. Men asked Jesus for restoration in their marriages. Others asked for forgiveness from someone else in the room. It was the most powerful prayer time to that point. As we wrapped up and wiped our eyes, one of the men in the room pulled out his phone's Bible app.

"I feel some of you need to hear this scripture deep in your bones today. It's from Isaiah 54:17– hear these words today."

"'No weapon forged against you will prevail, and you will refute every tongue that accuses you. This is the heritage of the servants of the LORD, and this is their vindication from me,' declares the LORD."

Before the call from HR, there was an average of fewer than ten people in my office on a Friday. However, after that Friday, more than twenty to twenty-five came for prayer and emotional healing. What someone meant for evil, God was turning into his good. It is not my job to get upset and try to defend God. He can defend himself. My job is to be faithful with what he has given to me. If you want to see a revival inside of your business or place of work, look first at the place where God has placed you. He won't send you on a mission without preparing the way ahead of you. Are you willing?

Honestly, writing this chapter, I had to search my heart again– five years later. I had to make sure I was willing to continue to forgive. Forgiveness is not a one and done like in the movies. It may be something that you have to continue to do, but the battle belongs to Jesus. To this day, I start every Friday standing next to the coin someone gave to my HR team. It sits on my desk as a reminder of God's grace and forgiveness for me, that what we are doing has a much greater purpose, and to press on, pray, and rejoice always. Lastly, it also reminds me that if I had given up, then almost one hundred people might not know Jesus today.

In living this chapter out, I learned several valuable lessons. These can be summarized as strength, honor, and courage. When a person you consider to be a friend turns on you, it will require a deep conviction filled with *strength* to press forward. I knew I was called to "Go Make Disciples," but I did not realize until now that my reaction was the "Go." I could have thrown a tantrum and made sure everyone in my department and building knew I was treated unfairly; however, the strength to pray anyway, love anyway, and be an example anyway was a valuable lesson. Where would the people who came to know Christ after that HR event be now if I had not had the strength to press on?

In whatever role you play at your workplace, whether leadership, mid-level management, or working at the entry-level, honor is a lesson of great importance. To be a part of a business revival and see the movement cascade across your organization, you must learn to honor the authorities placed around you. I honored my human resource team. They are there to protect and serve every organization. Honoring is not cowardly. Honoring is not shameful. Honoring all those around you is one of the fastest ways to see a revival. Looking back now, I can see the Lord protecting His movement by reminding me to honor those who work with and for me. I see a simple "this is optional" as a way to honor those whose hearts need protecting until the Holy Spirit prepares them. Constantly surrounded by eager sales-people, I started to see how important this was. It would be far too easy for people to be pulled into our prayer time through coercion or a desire to get ahead rather than a genuine heart to pursue Jesus.

If I had not met with human resources, if I had not responded well, if I had not set and honored clear boundaries, then I am not sure if our revival would still be going today. If I had not had my meeting with human resources to remind me to honor early on would our revival still be going strong? Or would it have been stopped?

Lastly, this chapter highlights the spark needed for all great revivals—*courage*. This small fire inside the soul of any person, when harnessed properly, can ignite the passions and purposes buried deep. This is also the place where most great movements faulter. For the next business revival to take place in the world, men and women will have to have the courage to walk out their faith, not in a pushy manner, but rather in the mundane and simple. Do you have enough courage to stand up to human resources for your faith? Most of us would immediately answer "YES!" However, the real question is, do you have enough courage to follow the rules and regulations of your company and lead people to Christ by the way you live? You don't have to be an outspoken weirdo to show up on time and work hard, nor do you need scripture and crosses on your wall to lead someone to Christ. No, what you need is courage to walk out your faith day in and day out: to pray when people ask for it, to love the people wanting your job. Courage is easily seen during the firecracker moments but is often neglected in the daily routines. To spark your business revival, you will need strength, honor, and courage.

Chapter 7

SECOND SERVICE

*I used to think agreement was needed to honor someone well.
Now, I know the greatest lessons of honor are birthed from
disagreements.*

"You got a minute?"

I dread these four words for multiple reasons: 1) It's never "a
minute," 2) No one needs just "a minute" for anything good, and 3)
Rarely can you say no to this request because the person needing a
minute already has their leader or person of interest cornered.

I responded like normal, "Sure, what's up?"

"You know in your little prayer group thingy that you have hourly employees, right?"

"What are you asking me?" I frowned.

Trapped between an obvious agenda and the time it takes for
me to rush to my next meeting, I paused and waited for the person
I respected greatly to respond. My heart was torn between "Is this
person looking out for me?" and "Why is this person telling me this
now?" Nonetheless, I listened to their concerns and tried not to
react.

"Brandon, they are in here stealing time from the company to do religious stuff. If I were you, I would want someone to make me aware. Look, I am in here as a friend because I don't want you to be surprised by anything." My friend stressed the point.

"Why are you telling me this today? I squinted.

"I just thought you should know. I heard a couple other VPs talking about it but please don't ask me which ones."

I needed to run off to my next meeting. My friend opened the office door and ended the conversation with the usual office jargon, "But you didn't hear this from me, right?" I nodded and strutted down the hallway. With a mixture of emotions swirling through me on the way to my next meeting, I let my mind travel in all directions. Why do they care? Am I really doing something wrong? Is this just jealousy because my teams are on top? Nevertheless, I finished my day, and Friday morning prayer happened the next morning like it had for nearly a year. I remember so clearly that we had more people that Friday than ever before. There were more new faces and more hourly employees. It was also the first time I closed with a challenge:

"Y'all, I want to challenge you this next month. Take a second and think about where God has placed you in this company. Who is in the office or cubicle next to you? My challenge is this: place your hand on the wall of those offices or cubes once a day on all sides and pray for those people. But don't let them know you are doing it. Pray from your place. Pray for their success, their family, and healing. Let's see the God we serve move!"

With laughter, grimaces, and groans, everyone nodded and joked about those they had been placed beside. However, as the grunts and jokes silenced, a clarity set into our meeting. A new vision, purpose, and perspective had been set before us.

However, about three o'clock in the afternoon I got a knock from my HR director at the time. She quickly cut the small talk and closed my office door behind her. In a quick gesture, she headed straight for my desk and pulled out a chair.

"Brandon, it has come to my attention that you have prayer on

Fridays in your office and you have hourly employees in here. Is that right?" She flopped into the chair.

"If you are asking if I pray in my office on Fridays and people come in on their own accord, then the answer is yes."

"Are there hourly employees?" she replied in annoyance.

"Yes, some. Is that an issue?" I frowned.

"Yes, they are in essence being paid to participate in religious activities because they are clocked in to do their jobs."

"Don't we allow smoke breaks and regular breaks for hourly employees?"

She inhaled deeply and replied, "Yes, but this is the first thing in the morning, right?"

"What does that matter? If they want to go smoke at eight o'clock, we let them, don't we? Or what if we told them not to clock in until eight-thirty?" I instantly blurted.

I could see the salesman inside of me starting to frustrate my human resources partner. Therefore, I slowly backed off and began to listen with the intent to understand instead of listening to respond. My friend warning me the day before had given me time to internalize and prepare my snarky response, but was that the real goal? If I pressed harder, I could win the battle, but the war for souls in our company was far greater than my need to be right. I make a living selling and teaching others to sell in tough situations, but my new task was to honor my company's wishes, not sell them on my beliefs. Two scriptures spoke directly to me in this exact moment in my life (Matthew 22:18-21, Romans 13:1).

"But Jesus, knowing their evil intent, said, 'You hypocrites, why are you trying to trap me? Show me the coin used for paying the tax.' They brought him a denarius, and he asked them, 'Whose image is on this? And whose inscription?' 'Caesar's,' they replied. Then he said to them, 'So give Caesar what is Caesar's, and to God what is God's.'" Matthew 22:18-21

"Let everyone be subject to the governing authorities, for there is no authority except that which God has established. The authorities that exist have been established by God." Romans 13:1 NIV

I did not need to go toe-to-toe with human resources to "get my way"; rather, I needed to pause, listen, and honor. Did I know what this would do to the folks coming on Friday? No. Did I know why this was brought to HR? No. Was I hurt and frustrated? Yes. Did I need to honor the request and see what Papa-God could do with the chaos? Absolutely.

"So, are you okay if the hourly employees want to come in before work on Fridays? I pray twice on Friday's sometimes. It's still me praying in my office, completely optional," I asked.

"If you are praying, and it is not a requirement and before work hours, that is up to you if you want to allow people into your time and office. But it needs to follow the company guidelines and handbook completely, just like it does at eight o'clock. Brandon, I am not a fan of this but if it follows policy and guidelines then it is fine," she firmly replied.

"Can you put that in an email to me, please? I just want to honor this place well and want to make sure I am completely above board." I stood from behind my desk.

"Yes, I will also copy your direct report. I would like for you to let your team know what is expected as well, please."

I nodded quickly.

I took the weekend to pour over my team in prayer and wait on wisdom from Papa-God. As Monday rolled around, I went to each hourly employee and told them the next expectation. I made sure to let them know that I would be available that Friday at seven thirty if they still wanted to pray. I received many emotional and even irrational responses. Some team members took the news well while others responded in instant anger.

This was a test of my leadership. I responded to each and every one that I agreed with our partners in human resources. They are not our enemy, and in fact they are the very protectors over organizations in this country. The roles and functions of this sales department are so much greater when we partner with our team in HR. (Hear me in this, reader; this is an important statement: HR is not the villain of this book or chapter. I still agree completely with this conversation. To start a business revival, you have to honor your company's wishes and protect its employees. When you honor well, God moves greatly.)

Up to this point, only about eight to ten hourly employees had shown up on a Friday and never at the same time. However, that next Friday morning, seven people were in the hallway waiting for me.

"Mornin'!" I grinned widely.

As the hallway crew followed me into my office, several more people came bounding down the hallway. A few of the faces were salary employees who wanted to show their support and join in with the earlier time. As we started to pray, I counted more than twenty-five people crammed inside. I was overwhelmed by the goodness of God. Once we wrapped up, I looked out the window facing the hallway, and multiple people who hadn't made it to seven-thirty prayer were now marching my direction. With bodies pouring into my office, several people asked, "Did we miss prayer already?" "Nope, come on in."

I watched and counted as new faces came marching into my office. At this point my office was overheating with almost thirty people shoved into the corners. As I started to pray, emotion overtook my soul. I looked around the room and addressed the faces with a shaky voice.

"Some of you may know, but this week I was asked that hourly employees not attend during this time. Through some hesitation and trepidation, I complied. I had no idea what God was going to do. My lack of faith made me wonder if we would even be able to continue. Not only are we continuing, but today we've had more people crammed into this office than ever before -- twenty-five earlier and almost thirty now. Look around you -- there is no physical way to have more than fifty people in here at one time! But God knew better!" I stood in amazement.

"We have two services now!" My friend Gary Landon grinned wildly.

As laughter reverberated off the office walls, I reached over to my computer and simply played a couple of worship songs to worship a God who is never surprised or caught off guard. Hands raised, the Spirit of God moved. Two-services were born.

(Five Years Later- we still meet at 7:30 and 8:00)

Chapter 8

BE A P.E.S.T.

I used to think I had to be weird to lead people to Jesus.
Now I know, I just need to be a PEST and HE will do the rest.

In the infancy of our business revival, I can remember being awakened early one morning. There was a beautiful thunderstorm booming outside, and the lightning crisscrossed the sky with reckless precision. I pulled myself out of bed quietly so as not to wake my pregnant wife. Gently gliding down the hallway, I watched the flashes of light effortlessly illuminate the house. I eventually made my way to the cold brick mud-room walkway and stared upward through the glass door. As I stood amazed for multiple minutes, I pulled the door open and sat under the overhang outside.

"Lord, what do you have for me this morning," I mumbled.

While the crisp fall storm danced playfully for me to enjoy, I sat calmly and continued to ask God for direction. What do I do about the work you have given to me? Is prayer just meant to be me and Gary? Who am I here for? What am I here for, Lord? We pray when people ask, but is that enough? Do I have what it takes to be successful at this company? What is a second baby going to do to the mix? I let my mind pour out all of the questions I could muster.

At that moment, I suddenly saw my lifelong gardening nemesis—a squirrel. I watched the furry guy run across my roof and leap into our pecan tree. At first, I was amazed the squirrel was out in the rain, and I grew fascinated by the specific yet random movements he made. It looked like he was running around without a plan, but every time he stopped, he found buried treasure! It was remarkable. It was also a little frustrating to watch him dig up my grass.

"Brandon, I want you to be like this squirrel."

I tried to shake off the still small voice in my mind by looking back to the clouds. The rain had come to a halt, and the sky slowly started to brighten as I walked back inside to prepare for my day. But my normal morning routine was continually interrupted by mental images of lightning and the squirrel. All the way to work and halfway through my morning calls, I still could not shake the morning squirrel out of my mind.

"What is it about the squirrel you want me to be like?" I mumbled to myself.

In that moment, I was grateful to have an office with the door closed. If not, I would have become the office nut-job: "There's mumble squirrel boy!" Finally, I gave up, grabbed a piece of paper, and started to write the characteristics of a squirrel. Furry. Soft. Good jumper. Squirrels seemed to always be around other squirrels. I was not progressing the way I thought I would.

"Hey, Bro. What's up! What you are doing?" My friend Gary popped my door open.

I quickly flipped over the paper and confidently replied like any man of God would have... "Nothing!"

Gary wasn't buying it. He looked at my paper on my desk and pressed forward. "What's that?"

I self-consciously flipped the yellow note pad back over and repeated "Nothing" once more. It dawned on me that I was trapped inside one of the very first lies experienced in the garden of Eden, asking, "Did God really say . . .?"

With one more probe into my squirming, Gary asked the same question in a different way: "What are you writing?" We are both trained to ask the same question multiple ways to verify truth. For example, when selling a franchise, we ask how much money a potential customer made in the past year. The person often replies, "Six figures." We then follow up by asking whether that was $100,000 or $900,000. (If you need a sales tip, "six figures" normally means between $90,000 and $130,000). Gary wasn't going to accept my vague reply, so I finally gave in.

"I'm just writing down this crazy idea I think God put on my heart, but I'm confused," I responded.

"What is it?" He didn't back off.

As I slowly unpacked the morning's events to Gary, he listened and offered some words to describe squirrels as well. Hard-working. Playful. Everywhere and nowhere. I added his comments to the running list. As Gary was leaving my office, he turned and jokingly gave one last answer.

"Maybe God wants you to be a PEST! Squirrels make me crazy." He chuckled.

"Me too! Tree-Rats!"

With the door closed and Gary laughing down the hallway, I looked down at my list and wrote P. E. S. T. As I turned to make the next scheduled call, I looked back at the list and waited for someone to answer. My eyes ran over the word "pest" several times and it was then that I again heard the still small voice whisper, "Exactly." No one answered. I picked up the notepad and noticed I had turned it into an acronym.

"P...E...S...T," I mumbled.

In a matter of minutes, I had the words to the acronym captured besides each letter. Prayer, Excellence, Strength, and Truth. I took an early lunch and walked down toward the river beside our offices. As I strolled beside the water, I carefully unpacked every word and how it pertained to the *business revival* I wanted to see take place.

*

PRAYER

As I unpacked the word Prayer, I asked God to remove the "churchy" stuff I had place inside my mind. I know what the word means, but how does this translate in the business world? The words the disciples spoke to Jesus flashed back through my mind, "Teach us to pray," (Luke 11:1). Like the disciples, I knew how to pray. I knew the mechanics of praying. I knew the words. But I knew there was so much more.

"It's relationship with me, Brandon," God's still small voice suddenly cut through my mind.

In an instant, another scripture penetrated my heart in a fresh way: "Rejoice always, pray continually, give thanks in all circumstances; for this is God's will for you in Christ Jesus," (1 Thessalonians 5:16-18).

"Brandon, I want you to talk with me about everything. It's like when you come home to your wife after work—prayer is telling me about your day. Tell me about it before it starts, in the middle of the day, and at the end."

I began to realize that praying without ceasing is about relationship, not perfect phrases that end with an "Amen." "Lord, I have this meeting today and I need help." "Lord, that meeting went terribly—help me understand why." "Papa, the people in this office need you. Help me to be present and ready when you send them to me." "Lord, send me the guy in our office going through things he doesn't want us to know." "Lord, who has sickness in their family that I can pray for? Will you send them to me?" I had spent my entire life approaching prayer like a daily wish list. In this simple walk, I saw it differently for the first time.

*

EXCELLENCE

Some Christians are eager to proclaim Christ and prayer but are hindered by excellence, or, more precisely, the lack thereof. I know some Christian employers who refuse to hire this type of "radical" Christian because they do not take their work seriously. In my current role as a senior executive, I am both frustrated and fascinated by what I see. Many brothers and sisters in Christ will happily profess "Send me, Lord!" They will gladly tell you, "I will go if the Lord calls me to the far reaches of the earth!" I wonder if God is instead calling them to show up on time for work or perhaps to keep their lunch hour to an actual hour. I worry they are missing out on His mission, the one right in front of them.

"Brandon, I want you to approach this mission like everyone is watching, because they are," I again discerned the Spirit speaking to my heart.

I had to reach deep inside and take an inventory of my life. Was I different? Was what is on the inside showing on the outside? Where were the places in my work that were "no big deal"? Was I living the standards I was asking my team to live?

Excellence is viewing work as a sacred calling. It is a commitment to be faithful, even in the little and mundane requirements of a job. It is the choice to live with integrity regardless of the culture of the rest of the office. Excellence doesn't mean you will always be the best, but it instead calls you to give your best. Excellence earns you the respect of people. They watch your life far more than they listen to your words.

Excellence cannot be cheated. There is not a short-cut to excellence. This is the place where promotions happen and differences are made. Excellence is the path less traveled. A business revival happens with a thousand simple tasks performed excellently over and over. I had heard, "Work unto, the Lord" from the pulpit so many times that it had lost its meaning. My entire working life, I have been surrounded by Christians in the workplace but have only seen a few who were different. Not many are truly "working unto the Lord."

"Papa, how do I do this and not be the weirdo?" I begged.

"Brandon, I am not asking for perfection, just consistency." Excellence is a muscle that is developed over time. Picture excellence as the tiny rudder to the massive ship of your life. A simple turn of one tiny degree won't seem like much at first. However, one simple choice, like a commitment to arrive on time, can shift your entire life's course. I wanted to make a difference, not just a mortgage payment, and this is often the deciding factor.

✳

STRENGTH

I believe strength follows excellence. Excellence is required to perform at a high level in any career, but strength is required to continue. By choosing the path less traveled, I also needed to develop the character to keep going. This is the place where continued prayer, excellence, and truth press against the insides of a person.

In a high-pressure environment, you have a choice to ask this simple question over and over: "What and who am I here for?" I realized that morning, and more so since then, that the daily grind is part of the mission field. You need strength after the missed business opportunity, the wear-and-tear of office politics, and irrational customers. This is true of any workplace, but especially for those who contend for a business revival.

The strength to keep going is where most people fail. The greatest movements happen on the other side of where most people quit. To maintain this strength, we need to tap into the strength of Jesus. We need to recognize that it is Him—His presence and leadership— who empowers us to keep going.

As I pondered strength, I sensed God speak to my heart, "Brandon, you keep asking me to send you everywhere except where I have already placed you. The breakthrough is in the current mission you are on." I wanted to take the easy path and go back into the industry I had come from. My old career was easier: I knew the industry, and I knew how to make more money. In that moment, I asked God to give me the strength to continue. I knew this strength to continue wasn't going to come from me.

I felt God's leadership as He brought to mind one of my favorite quotes. "Brandon, there is a mission and a task I have set for you in this company. You were built for this; you are the man in the arena."

"It is not the critic who counts. Not the man who points out how the strong man stumbles or where the doer of deeds could have done them better. The credit belongs to the man who is actually in the arena, whose face is marred by dust and sweat and blood, who strives valiantly, who errs, who comes short again and again, because there is no effort without error and shortcoming; but who does actually strive to do the deeds, who knows great enthusiasms, the great devotions, who spends himself in a worthy cause, who at best knows in the end the triumph of high achievement, and who at the worst, if he fails, at least fails while daring greatly, so that his place shall never be with those cold and timid souls who neither know victory nor defeat."

Theodore Roosevelt, "The Man in the Arena," *Citizen in a Republic Speech*, April 23, 1920

TRUTH

Integrity is the area tested the most and where you cannot waiver. Integrity is who you are when no one is around and when no one knows.

Integrity recognizes that omitting a piece of information is still not being honest. It chooses to give back an accounting mistake in your favor. It is recognizing a cashier charged you the wrong price and, rather than considering it a discount, asking them to verify. I did not realize it until recently, but truth and integrity are the places where I have been tested the most. Integrity is also where I have seen many Christians falter. It is easy to fight for the side of truth when a wrong has been done to us. But are you willing to fight for truth when the chips all fall in your favor? Can you call yourself a person of integrity if you are teaching dishonest sales or management practices? Truth is the glue that ties the P.E.S.T together. It is the place where true relationship with God in prayer happens. I often ask, "Papa, what do I do? Is this a blessing or a testing?"

I have seen countless professionals in my career who would call themselves people of truth, but their actions say otherwise. Truth challenges us to go the other way and not follow everyone else's path. If you want to see a business revival, you have to start by making daily decisions against yourself. You must truly search out the circumstance you are in and know the truth.

"Consider it great joy, my brothers and sisters, whenever you experience various trials, because you know the testing of your faith produces endurance. And let endurance have its full effect, so that that you may be mature and complete, lacking nothing." James 1:2-4

*

I will never forget the simplicity of the challenge given to me to live like a squirrel, even though living as a P.E.S.T is still a constant work in progress in my life. We've witnessed more than one hundred people surrender their lives to Jesus in our workplace, and almost every single conversation starts with the same words:

"I don't know what it is about y'all, but I want in. What you have is different. I have tried it my way and it isn't working. I want the Jesus I see in your lives."

A business revival is an invitation to get what is inside you inside your company. This prompts the question: What is inside of you? Do you truly pray? Is your work excellent? Do you persevere in the strength of God? Does your life reflect a commitment to truth? This starts with a commitment. We are all on a journey of spiritual growth, but what is your destination? Let's resolve together to be a PEST.

P.S. I still don't like squirrels

Chapter 9

HANDS AGAINST THE WALL

I used to think this was only a saying from my past;
Now, I know it's the simplest prayer weapon to teach.

The prayer crew rolled into my office like any other Friday morning. New and familiar faces moved into the circle, and I reminded the group that this meeting was optional. As I spoke, I heard the still small voice whispering "I placed you here for such a time as this."

The small talk and gentle laughs echoed around my office. Nonetheless, the phrase flashed again like a beacon inside my soul. I reached for my computer to play a simple worship song. Once the song had finished, the room was silent and at peace.

"Close your eyes for a second. Think about the co-workers God has placed on all sides of you in offices or cubes at work. Now think about the needs they have in their lives. Maybe they are struggling in sales, or their family is having challenges, or they have been ill. Maybe you have had even issues with that person...." I paused. "You know what? Maybe they bounce that ridiculous squishy ball against your wall—pray Jesus would help them lose that absurd thing!" The room laughed knowing this was my pet peeve. "Keep your eyes closed. Focus on your prayers for each person. Truly, search to see why God placed that person next to you. If *you need to say, "I'm sorry," do it!* I want to challenge you to place your hand on the wall of their offices or cubes once a day and pray for those people, but don't let them know you are doing it. Watch Papa-God bring healing with your willingness and brokenness."

I am not sure what made me say this challenge. There is a part of me that wants to blame Mark Batterson's book, *The Circle Maker*, but more so, it was the still small whisper that continued all the way through the song. Goosebumps rose instantly on my skin as I issued the challenge. I knew this was not something I had conjured on a whim.

With a new vision cast and a purpose put into perspective, the room slowly responded. One of the more seasoned salesmen quickly responded, "Wow, guys. This is so good. The person in the office next to me is the most annoying neighbor I have had here in the last ten years. No, seriously. It never hit me until today that just maybe God put them in that office for me to pray for them."

"Guys, this is easy. We can do this," another voice spoke.

As the room emptied, several of the sales professionals made sure to stop and challenge me back. Even though the squishy ball jokes were laced with sarcasm, I felt a tug inside me to take the mission. Therefore, over the next several days I pressed my hand against the wall of the ball bouncer. More than once, the ball bouncing only happened as my hand was pressed along his wall. I had brothers in Christ praying for the healing of people with cancer, while I just wanted Jesus to stop a ball from crashing incessantly against my office wall. I even tried to take matters into my own hands and snuck into the office next to me and threw the ball away multiple times, but it was to no avail. I work for a company that gives them away by the truck load. One can never have too many stress balls to create stress for your neighbor.

*

For the next month, I reminded the people coming into Friday prayer to pray for the people on all sides. In most cases, the relationship or prayer request became harder—not just for me and the ball bouncer but for everyone. Therefore, "game time" adjustments had to be made. I had been waiting for the one-month mark, but when it finally came, we had still not seen any "results"—no changes, miracles, salvations, healings, or even a lost ball. "Papa, what do I do?" I mumbled to myself.

The toughest part in any move of God is the space between breakthrough and giving up. The *just a little more* space. The *one more time around* truth. In these moments, I lean into a piece of advice my late mentor Calvin B. Petersen gave me years ago, "Are you interested in seeing this come to pass, or are you committed to it? The difference between interest and commitment is razor thin...but the difference separates generations sharper than a razor's edge." Another quote I keep on my desk is from Wade Cook and states: *"If you choose to do what others refuse to do for just a short while, then you can do what they cannot do for the rest of your life."*

In the month after the challenge was issued, I was asked to stop praying in my office by HR. I had to fire two team members on the same three-person team for ethical reasons. My house was battling sickness. The ball bouncer continued. The entire department's sales hit the bottom. However, I continued to challenge the crew and myself to press onward and upward. The joy of walking the hallway through the day and seeing hands pressed against conjoining walls was overwhelming, but now it was something deeper. When opposition comes while praying, then it's time to press harder.

"Y'all, let's keep pushing for another month. This time, if you see someone praying for their neighbor, ask if you can join. I will do the same if I see you. Also, if you are chatting in each other's offices, ask each other if you have prayed for your neighbors. If not, do it right there. Don't dawdle. Pop in, pray, high five, and then go sell something. Let's join together while also being respectful each other and our time. *We are the underground church in America.*"

For the next several weeks, I saw the team alone and in pairs, and with their hands pressed against the sheetrock. From time to time, I popped in and joined, in order to remind them this is everyone's battle (and to make sure some weren't just hanging out). The sense of adventure and secrecy almost became a game. When an office or a cubical opened up, I had team members ask if I could help them get the new location so they could pray for the people on either side. It was amazing to have team members wanting a smaller office, without a window or giving up their window, to be closer to someone they wanted to pray for.

We persisted for many more weeks, and that's when it happened. It was the moment when I knew God was absolutely in our prayers.

Knock, Knock.

"Come on in. What's up? You're here early, huh?" I joked with my neighbor.

"Yeah, I came in hoping to find you." He nervously squeezed his yellow stress ball.

"For sure. Everything okay?"

The man sliding onto my office furniture was one of our best sales professionals. He was not on one of my teams, but he and I held tons of respect for one another. We joked back and forth about his ball bouncing and his choice of college football team, but never anything truly serious. Yet, today I could see a glint of pain in his eyes.

"Yeah, um...I know you pray in here on Fridays and stuff. Will you pray for me? Just a lot going on, you know?" He paused and looked at the floor.

"Sure. Do you want to be more specific? Anything particular?" I gently responded.

Without saying a word, I waited patiently. He looked up and

down several times, and I stayed silent. He was already out of his comfort zone, but I knew he didn't need the Christian guy next to him solving his problems with a bunch of churchy words. I believe most Christians are so eager to help that they run to their knowledge about God before they wait on God or run to God, the giver of knowledge.

"Everything is just falling apart, B. Mom is really sick with cancer, my sales are in the toilet, me and the old lady are fighting about everything. The kids are making us crazy. I mean you name it. I've got this crazy neighbor who smiles through my window and waves ridiculously every time I bounce this ball to numb out a bit!" He wiped his cheeks and chuckled at my expense.

"First, tell me your mom's name so that I can pray for her."

He quickly told me and wiped more tears.

"Second, if you keep calling your wife 'my old lady,' it ain't going to get better, so stop it!" I grinned and then began to encourage him about sales and being a dad.

"This is exactly why I woke up early. It's good to talk about it."

"Well, talking is good, but let's pray too." I patted his knee and prayed.

As we finished praying, my neighbor popped up from his chair, hugged me tightly and headed out the door.

"Hey! You left your squishy ball," I shouted as the door shut.

"You keep it." He winked.

"IN JESUS NAME!" I shouted through the window.

That same week, seven weeks after the original challenge, several more people reported back with powerful stories. Each one had the same "random knock" at the door. As we met to pray and share in the thanksgiving of God's goodness, everyone in the room became overwhelmed with hope. What had started as a secretive prayer challenge had now become something deeper inside our hearts and our company.

I still love to walk around the building and see men and women praying or sitting against the walls connecting to their offices. The simplicity of praying inside your own space, for those placed next to you, has taken off across the entire campus. I hear stories of people moving in and around the different buildings praying "in secret."

The challenge is also for you today. Who are the people God has strategically placed in your life? Who are your neighbors? Can you lay a hand on the walls between you and a co-worker and pray? Can you place a hand on the fence dividing you?

PASTORAL PERSPECTIVE: CHRIST'S AMBASSADORS

Paul's second letter to the Corinthians is emotional and sometimes chaotic. It is also extremely relevant for us living in modern America. The apostle penned this epistle during a deeply painful conflict between him and the church. The dispute centered around one consistent theme: The Corinthians did not receive Paul's leadership because he did not meet their cultural standards for success. Sound familiar?

They expected leaders to have a dynamic personality and communicate with strength. In their view, leaders should climb the social ladder and seek out the appropriate credentials—apparently Paul didn't make the cut.

This situation sets the context for the entire letter. At the crux of Paul's reply is a challenge for the Corinthians and a challenge for us: We need to redefine life, success, and purpose through the lens of the cross and the example of Jesus.

God has given us a treasure, but it's found in jars of clay. We joyfully await a heavenly home but must first live faithfully in a human tent. At times we feel like we are wasting away, but God is renewing us every single day and imparting a confidence that cannot be shaken, even with a stock market crash or layoff.

This background sets the stage for 2 Corinthians 5:14-21 and its dynamic metaphor for Christian witness. The ministry of Jesus introduced a new Kingdom into the world. This Kingdom is radically different from the systems of this world—read Matthew 5-7 and consider the reality of each statement. It's as counter-cultural today as it was in the first century.

The Kingdom of God is active now. When we embrace the call of discipleship and follow Jesus, then we die to our old self and are reborn as members of Christ's Body and under His rule. The Holy Spirit is given as a direct deposit of our future inheritance. Every time we see God heal the sick, forgive the sinner, and deliver the afflicted we get a glimpse of His Kingdom.

However, God's Kingdom is also not yet. The world is still under the influence of evil. Sin is still operative in the human heart. The effect of sin's curse continues to plague the earth and all the systems of humanity. We live under the weight and pain of the not yet even as we celebrate the now.

As you consider all of this, I pray you grasp the significance of your job title: You are Christ's ambassador. An ambassador is the legal representative of one kingdom to another. Ambassador's very words carry the weight of the King. It's a high calling.

Your primary career is to be an ambassador, no matter your place on the flow chart or the job title on a business card. You represent the Kingdom of God everywhere you go. Your cubicle is an embassy of Heaven. Your life and actions point to another reality. I cannot think of a higher calling or more significant role.

The nature of this calling is holistic. The ministry of reconciling people to God is central to the role but the role cannot be reduced to words alone. Does your work ethic reflect your Kingdom identity or your paycheck? Do your values align with the teaching of Jesus or your corporate culture? Are you motivated by people or numbers? We need a fundamental shift in our understanding of our calling.

Chapter 10

SEVEN AND COUNTING

*I used to simply think that children were a blessing from God;
Now I know they are an ANSWER TO PRAYER.*

"How you guys doing?" I smiled like normal.

"We are blessed...for the most part." His eyes became misty.

"What do mean?" I frowned.

As the smell of perfectly steamed rice and chicken yellow curry
floated magically through the restaurant, our waiter glided two fresh
glasses of water towards us.

"You guys ready to order?"

The waiter interrupted our conversation with zero empathy.
I asked for another minute, slid my silverware further to the right,
and placed my menu down. As I asked my friend to continue telling
me what "for the most part" looked like to him, I watched his body
language shift to defeat.

"I mean, I wouldn't say we're struggling. In fact, we are doing
great in almost every way possible. I mean, we are so blessed, you
know?" He lifted his menu to cover his face. "I mean, we...."

With my lips tightly closed to force awkward silence, I stayed
laser focused on my friend. For the next several minutes, I watched
the internal battle within him. One minute he was "blessed" and the

next the "struggle" was real. I simply listened. It didn't take a genius to see my friend bouncing in and out of "church speak"; he said a lot of words and nothing at all.

I hear a lot of church speak, phrases like "we are blessed," "God is good all the time," "just waiting on the Lord," and "His ways are not our ways," just to name a few. Unfortunately, these are often used to mask the reality of life's pain. I've learned to disregard this talk and push into the deeper issues. Often this simply looks like attentive listening and a few pointed questions. While all of what he had said is true, none of it brought him comfort, only more hiding.

"Bro, you have just said fifteen sermons, thirty-seven "we are blesseds," seasoned the entrée with a final "His ways aren't my ways," and I still have no idea what you are saying. Are you struggling with something or are you blessed?"

The confusion on my face caused my friend to laugh nervously. I believe what he needed was someone to ask him the hard question. Christians get so used to the Christian "jargon" that we forget sometimes that it is okay to hurt and be "real." The greatest gift I could give my friend was comfort and a safe place for the truth.

"Can I ask you another question? Why did you ask me to have lunch with you?" I cut to the chase.

"Ummm...." He swallowed hard. "I was telling my wife about how you have prayer in your office on Fridays, and I have heard that several of the people who attend, like us, were told they couldn't have children, and, well, we have been trying for several years. Could you pray for us?" My friend's eyes filled with tears.

In that exact moment, tears in both of our eyes, our waiter returned. Apparently, he had the best timing on the planet. The two of us wiped our faces, ordered the yellow curry, and cleared our throats like men. I reached across the table and held out my hand. My friend, looking confused, grabbed my paw. He quickly realized we were about to pray in the middle of the busy Thai restaurant. But his desperation outweighed his social concern and placed him in front of another who wasn't afraid.

Once we finished praying, he quickly thanked me and, without prompting, told me of their years of struggles. I listened to my friend and asked a series of questions. I did not try to solve his problems. I didn't say, "I understand." I listened, and when it was appropriate, I said, "I'm so sorry," or "Man, that sucks." Too many times, when someone needs our ears, we give them our mouth. What my friend needed was someone to listen and not try to "fix" anything. As we finished up our lunch, I told my friend he was welcome to join our optional prayer on Friday. I stuck out my hand for a handshake, and he quickly gave me a bear hug.

Later that week, my friend timidly walked into my office to join about twenty other people for prayer. The others were surprised and excited to see the new face. I felt led to play a certain song and ask the group to close their eyes and listen to the words. Breaking my own rule, I opened my eyes and scanned the room. Both of the men for whom we had prayed to have children after being told they couldn't were standing in the room. I knew in that moment Papa God was up to something.

"All right, good morning. As we get going, like we always do, I want to remind you that this is optional. This is me praying in my office and you don't have to be here. You chose to walk down here." I smiled at the gentle grins around the cramped office.

Each of us stated our moments of gratitude from this past week and a prayer request. Since my friend was standing to my right, I went first and asked the person to my left to go next. I could see my friend's nervousness; however, I watched the nerves quickly fade when a person two or three more people around the circle began to speak:

"Yeah, I am thankful that God's goodness to me supersedes

my own unbelief. We have a beautiful baby on the way thanks to the prayers in this office and a God who is SO faithful. Many of you know, but I feel like I am supposed to say it again for some reason: we were told we could not have kids, we tried Invitro twice, we looked at adoption—all of it. BUT God brought the breakthrough."

I watched the tears well up inside my friend, so I gently patted him on the shoulder and called the next person's name. The circle continued, person by person, submitting thanksgiving and prayer requests to God. Then it was finally his turn.

"Um, yeah, so I guess it's my turn" he started. "We have been trying to get pregnant for more than five years. I want y'all to pray for me and my wife."

With emotion taking over, my friend ended his request and rubbed his sweaty palms against his black slacks. Before I could say anything at all, the man who had just praised God for the child in his wife's womb spoke to my friend:

"What's the baby's name?" He grinned in my direction. A few months earlier, this man had been standing in my office with the same desperation and the same question had been posed to him.

My friend frowned. "What? We are still trying to get pregnant."

In an instant, the spiritual and the physical worlds inside my friend's mind crashed together like a high-speed collision. As the explanation of the question unfolded, I watched the proverbial light bulb inside my friend's soul begin to glow. It did not take long for the names he and his wife had chosen, for either boy or girl, to come out. With the group swiftly locking arms to pray, I gripped my friend by the bicep. While I prayed with desperation over the broken man, it was easy to hear the sobbing of two names repeatedly. As the loud cries in the circle became gentle murmurs, I wrapped up the prayer and asked my friend to step into the center of the circle.

"Okay, y'all. Put your hand on our brother, and if this was you, how would you want people to pray for you if you and your wife had been seeking for years? Let's pray for the exact names he said and cover him in prayer!"

After praying, the group gave hugs and swiftly went back to work. My friend paused and waited to be the last one to leave. Gently wiping his face, he sauntered back over to give me a hug.

"That was awesome. I have never...I mean, where did that come from?" He pushed his pressed shirt across his cheeks.

"Either God is who He says He is or not. I choose to believe He is the God who gives life to the dead and calls into being things that are not. There isn't anything special about this group or these people—it's all Jesus—we just have to make space to let him do his thing."

While my friend was slowly walking back out into the hallway, I gave him a challenge. I told him to go home and pray together with his wife for thirty straight days. I encouraged them to give thanks for the other couples who have seen a miracle, even as they still waited for a breakthrough in their own lives.

Not everyone sees the miracle they are believing for. We've seen prayer answered miraculously, and, for others, we continue to contend for breakthrough. The issue is faith and the belief that God is able to move, to heal, and to restore. Like the parable of the persistent widow, this faith causes us to keep showing up and asking God to move. And you know what? He consistently does.

As of the time of writing this, seven couples who have been told they could not have children now all have children. My friend from this chapter? God answered his prayers and he is now a proud papa. God has shown himself faithful.

"The tongue has the power of Life and Death, and those who love it will eat of its fruit." Proverbs 18:21 (NIV)

"... in the presence of the God in whom he [Abraham] believed, the God who gives life to the dead and calls into being things that were not." Romans 4:17 (NIV)

Chapter 11

DE-TERMINATION

I used to think when people were terminated for lack of performance they stayed gone. Now I am convinced, if they are loved and led well, they will return.

Terminating employees is one of the worst responsibilities for a leader. Most managers are not prepared for this responsibility, and there is no way to call firing anyone a success, but it is part of every company, especially in high-performance sales. Throughout my decade of executive leadership, I have been a part of these conversations more times than I can count. I remember each one vividly, though none more clearly than the first.

It was a normal Friday afternoon; the first quarter had just ended in an exemplary fashion. I entered my boss' office for a normal meeting, and his eyes stayed fixed on his computer. As I pulled the chair out to take a seat, he shouted politely to his assistant to bring "us" the final sales statistics "broken down per sales professional." While we bantered small talk back and forth, I could hear the pages he requested printing rapidly.

"Here you guys go. Anything else?" his assistant popped in pleasantly.

As my boss, my present-day mentor, took his seat next to me, he quickly flipped through the pages of the report. "Do you have the list of any current performance improvement plans (PIP) outstanding?"

"No, sir. I'll go get it."

I dashed back to my office, grabbed the documentation and returned. He and I carefully matched the report of PIPs and final quarter statistics. After a few moments of looking over the total staff, seventy-plus sales professionals, we both identified the same issues.

"I just don't get it." He pointed to a sales professional's name on the page and continued. "I mean, he has all the talent in the world but something in his process is missing, or maybe he is just not following the process at all?"

"He's selling scared, which causes him not to follow the process. I mean, he is a great relationship builder, but he becomes slimy and pushy when it is time to close the deal," I shrugged.

"Why do you think that is? Are you helping with his closes?" my boss replied with a hint of accusation.

"Yes, sir. I am helping. However, even after a close, he hangs around and un-does all the relationship building by becoming force-ful. This is a massive breach of trust and would make any candidate pause. I think he does this because he desperately needs the money."

The employee in question was hired directly by the Executive Vice President before I took over the team. But my boss knew I was speaking truth. In fact, he knew this man in a deep personal and professional way. He knew my employee better than I did. He was his hire and his friend.

"Everything you just said is accurate. I have known him for decades. This is the worst part of the job, when you have great people that you must let go. He truly is a fantastic man, but we have been pretty clear in our expectations and have helped as much as possible, it sounds like." My boss shook his head.

After a few more minutes of discussion, my mentor went back around his desk and dialed Human Resources, the Information Tech-nology Department, and then the sales professional's extension. In a moment, there was a knock on the door and our HR representative entered, followed by the salesman. As the conversation about performance expectations unfolded, the gentleman asked a few clarifying questions and eventually received his termination notice. The IT department was notified to turn off his key card and access. Hands were shaken. Heaviness filled the air. I walked the salesman back to his office to gather his things.

As we entered the office, the salesman turned, "Brandon, I know this is tough. I was a leader of sales teams in a past life too, but I want you to know I have nothing but the utmost respect for you and your leadership."

"Same here. If I can do anything at all, you just let me know." I stuck out my hand.

Within thirty minutes, our administrative team and the salesman had placed his personal belongings into the back of his car. As he pulled out of the parking lot, I marched back down to the office manager's office and handed over his office keys and key card. The "How'd it go?" conversation quickly ended and I walked back into my office. My boss was already there waiting for me.

"You know, these are never easy, especially when it's someone who is a great person and someone you care about. But we did everything we could for him, Brandon. You led him well."
In the sobriety of the moment, I felt as though my boss was peering into my soul.

"Thank you."

A full week went by and I was in my office early the next Friday. I had just walked through the door and started a cup of coffee. Knock, knock. Looking up, my un-caffeinated brain received a jolt when I saw the recently fired employee.

"Hey, B. Can I come in?"

"Sure, what are you doing here?" I turned.

"Well, the new lady at the front desk let me in, so I thought I would pop by. By the way, somebody needs to train her better." He paused to chuckle and continued. "You guys still praying? I mean, I know I am early, right?"

Staring directly at this man I had just fired the week prior, I stood awestruck for a brief second. With a quick sip of fresh coffee, I told him to take a seat and offered him a cup. The gentle pleasantries lasted only a few minutes, as sales professionals entered my office with everyone smiling, hugging, or letting out a hearty "Hey!" to their former colleague. The room slowly filled to maximum capacity, and I felt the butterflies inside my stomach start to take off. For the last several months, I had opened the prayer by asking the room questions: What are you thankful for and who are you praying for this week?

Was I really going to ask the guy who had just been fired what he was thankful for? I forced the internal squirming to halt and prayed. I then asked if I could share a song before we began. The song filled the room with worship and simultaneously silenced the conversations. As we lifted hands in worship, I knew that I needed to set aside my awkwardness and ask the same questions I always do.

The worship came to a pause and I asked the normal questions, "What are you thankful for? Who are you crying out to God for this morning? Who do you want the spirit of God to fall on today? Who needs healing? Salvation? Marriage help?"

Immediately following the questions, I gave my answers and the person to my right gave his. We proceeded around the room until we got to the gentleman who had lost his job. He cleared his throat and stood from his chair. For a few seconds, he carefully looked around the room and tears began to fill his eyes.

"You know, it's easy for me to say what I am thankful for this morning. First, I am thankful for this group right here. Y'all have no idea what this group means to me. The people in this room have poured into me, loved me, and served alongside me tirelessly. My marriage is better, my walk with God is better, and I have complete peace for what is next because of the crew in here. Getting ready this morning I knew there was no way I was going to miss this. There was a holy determination inside my soul, and I knew right away this was where I was supposed to be. Secondly, I am so thankful for the goodness of God and for friends to challenge me and lead me back towards the goodness of God. I have been loved better in this office and led to Christ more in this building than a lifetime of anything else. Y'all keep it up. Lead each other, love on each other, and pray over one another. Miracles have happened here—new babies, cancers healed, salvations. What we do in this office is powerful. And Brandon, I am just gonna keep comin' so..." He paused and the room laughed.

As he paused and laughter broke into the moment, I watched a room full of sales professionals turn into the hands and feet of the church. He was immediately engulfed with hugs, pats on the back, amens, and tears.

It was in this very moment I saw the Great Commission in a whole new way. A man who had been terminated from employment was *de-termined* to be in the place he felt loved. His lack of sales performance had nothing to do with the surgical performance the Holy Spirit had done in his heart through his employment. His anemic spiritual life, which he freely confessed, had been transformed by walking and working alongside men and women who led him to Jesus. This man of God was not forced to come back to that prayer meeting; rather, the love of the believers drew him back.

✳

As I write five years later, this man still periodically attends our prayer meetings.

It is a story of God's goodness. Yes, he was terminated. But he went on to find a better paying job. He now leads a large team, and he is leading his own prayer meetings on Tuesday mornings where he, too, has seen the salvation of God, healings, and marriages restored. He and I have met several times to disciple these new believers. He also prayer walks around his building, lays hands on walls, prays on the spot, and leads people to Jesus.

During a virtual prayer meeting this past Friday, I looked carefully around the thirty-plus faces on the call. Four of the people attending the call had been terminated and returned to a virtual prayer meeting because they were loved well and met Jesus in a sales organization. You can conduct business and keep business standards. And you can love people well in the process. To do this, you must be *determined* to lead people to Jesus in success and in failures.

Chapter 12

MAXIMIZE YOUR LUNCH

I used to think leadership was the place to show how much you know; Now I know, it's the place to show how much you care.

Currently, I am blessed to have three wonderful sons: Hunter (Lion), Hagan (Tiger), and Hudson (Bear). These mighty warriors are constantly testing their strength on each other and on me. Swift kicks. Hard punches. Rough housing. Crazy wrestling moves. Karate skills. It's all part of the gig in the Haire house. There have been numerous times lately where an unsuspecting daddy (Dragon) gets "jacked-up" by a sneak attack.

"Oh, you want a piece of me, huh? You want a shot at the title?" I reply with a smile.

"We don't want a piece; we want the whole thing big boy!" they shout back in my direction.

With gut laughs and shrill screeches, my sons rush away from me, and we sprint to the playroom carpeted floor. I will always grab the closest Haire man swiftly, and gently pin the giggling warrior to the ground. As the unlucky closest opponent is tickled profusely, his counterpart will proceed to bounce all over daddy to free his brother. In doing so, he, too, will be pinned and trade places with his brother.

This continues until all three boys have joined the battle. If one is missing, I will cry out, "Where's your other brother? Come on Men! You will always be stronger together than you are apart!"

The Daddy-Dragon finally surrenders after he is attacked by all three together. My boys have now figured it out and have learned to call for their brothers to come to their aide. Truly, these are some of my favorite moments and memories. And this is the perfect picture of revival leadership. Let me explain.

As you are reading this chapter, I am just a few months away from having my black belt in *Tae Kwon Do*. I work out five days a week, and my sons are finishing second grade, kindergarten, and pre-school. I could easily defeat these boys. I am a grown man and they are still warriors in training. In these joyful times I choose to teach rather than dictate. I choose to participate rather than dominate. I choose to include rather than exclude. It is a beautiful thing to see those you are leading have a safe place to test their knowledge and strength. Are you a safe place for new ideas and challenges?

Leading people is similar. We can be competitive and challenge people, while also creating a safe environment for them. People need to know we care about them as people, not use them to accomplish our career goals.

I believe "Christian leadership" has become like the fake pockets on women's jeans. They look like pockets. They are in the right place. Still, at the end of a close examination, they are counterfeit. I believe this is what prevents a true business revival. It's not enough for a little scripture to decorate a dusty bookshelf. Our prayers should not be limited to closing deals. Too many people say they believe, yet they relegate their faith to a "private thing". How do we instead live out our faith in the workplace? Do those we work with see the love of Jesus in our lives? Below are a few questions I routinely ask the Christians I mentor:

- Looking at your life, how would I know you are a Christian if you didn't tell me?

- Are you interested in making a difference or committed to it?
- Tell me your story.
- What's the number one chore at home your spouse can't stand doing? Will you do it from now on? (If they are Married.)
- Inventory your life, where are places you want to be served more than you are willing to serve?
- Who in your workplace gets under your skin most? Will you pray for them for the next sixty days straight?
- What are you praying over your children or grandchildren in this season? (If they have children/grandchildren.)
- Why has God sent you into the current job or career you are in?
- What does your relationship with God look like?
- Does God feel near to you in this season or far away? Why?
- Are you willing to go anywhere God would send you and give it all you have until the task is done? Has He sent you here? And are you still willing?

There is a saying, "People don't care how much you know until they know how much you care." I wholeheartedly believe this saying, especially when it comes to leading teams. Do you see your team as a vehicle to get you to the next temporary success, or as a vessel to pour love, excellence, and truth into? If you want to lead people to Jesus and teach them to do likewise, then you must be present in their lives. I believe this is a place where we miss the opportunity.

Since my first son was born, my wife and I have had a standing Wednesday lunch in or around my office. We are located next to a beautiful park, so we often choose to go outside. In my previous career in banking, I could not bring my wife and family to the branch to eat with me. After she decided to stay home with Hunter and pause her amazing career as a Child Life Specialist, we realized we could take a break in the middle of the week to see each other.

Though this has evolved many times over the last decade, it is still the highlight of my week. One of the overwhelming benefits of having my family come to the office every Wednesday is that it has allowed people into my world. It has also created opportunities for me to show off as a proud daddy. I challenge everyone to ask any of my sons, "What do Haire men do?" to which one of my boys would confidently respond:

"We love God, love people, and change the world."

As my career progressed and my family continued to come on Wednesdays, it also made way for many other professionals to do likewise. It is the joy of my week to see families enjoying lunch together and new team members bring their families to my office for introductions. As a result, we've seen whole families come to know Jesus together. I love watching team members invite other families over for dinner and model for their children men and women honoring Jesus in the workplace. We've walked with families through painful situations, and we've seen God bring breakthrough in restoring marriages and other places of life's pain.

My current Executive Coach, Bill Moyer of SOS Leadership, has taught me one of his sayings. The four *knows* of Leadership: *Know* your people, *know* their goals, *know* what they are doing, and you will always *know* the results. I believe this foundational teaching from SOS Leadership is a key component to creating the business revival in the world today.

Know your people: Truly, know their story, their hearts, their lives, and their families.

Know their goals: Why are they here? What are your team members hoping to accomplish?

Know what they are doing: This is not micromanagement but getting into their lives. Are they taking their families camping? Do they have an anniversary or family member birthday coming up? Invest time in asking and caring about their lives.

Know the result: The result is loving people, serving them well, and caring about their outcome. All you must do is love people and let God open the opportunities to bring them to Him.

Chapter 13

COVID-19

*I used to think quarantine meant no way in or out; Now I know
Jesus is not restricted EVEN if the whole world is quarantined.*

As I am amid the writing of this book, the world is on high alert
for an unseen enemy. The Covid-19 virus, or Coronavirus, has taken
center stage on its world-wide tour. The New York Stock Exchange
dropped at record pace. In the town I call home, like most across
the country, restaurants, churches, bars, local businesses and most
places where people gather have all closed their doors. There is
uncertainty everywhere. Even the multi-billion-dollar corporation
where I am now a senior executive decided to take our one thousand
employees virtual. The world is scared, and the grocery store aisles
are bare. Most people made a mad dash to the toilet paper aisle as fast
as they could, even though symptoms don't cause people to need that
product.

This has become such an amazing moment for me to see the
journey the business revival must endure to succeed. For our nation
and our world to catch fire for Jesus, we must navigate an even more
desperate and deadly sickness in our culture—selfishness. I have witnessed and even caught myself taking part in mad dashes to stockpile

in preparation for the unknown. Firsthand accounts are everywhere. We are desperate to remain in some type of control. We quickly hide our goods, store our ammo, and shut the blinds to our windows.

How then can we see God move when our churches are reduced to streaming services? What about the helpless and hopeless? What about the millions of people who are not streaming live worship for a shot of hope? As I began to ponder these questions, I became fearful for our Friday prayer gathering, where almost one hundred people have come to know Christ. I prayed, "Lord, how do we meet? This is for you! Healings take place in our meeting, salvations, and so much more."

I spent several days in prayer, asking Papa-God to reveal a great mystery to me. "Lord, what am I here for, and who am I here for?" I went back to Matthew 28:19:

"Therefore go and make disciples of all the nations, baptizing them in the name of the Father and of the Son and of the Holy Spirit."

I read the scripture over and over. I had no idea why this was the scripture that kept racing through my mind. For three days, I heard this scripture in my mind, my dreams, and at random times. Even as I tried to forget it, I received a call from a friend of mine who owns two small home service business—one in Alabama and one in New York.

"Yo, B! Wonder what our Papa is up to, eh? The world says it's bad, but our God is bad-er, you hear me?" His thick New York accent resounded through the phone.

"Amen! How you doin' ov'a der?" I tried my best accent back.

"If y'all" -- he paused to make sure I heard "y'all" and then continued -- "can't see that this has the hand of God all ov'r it, someone needs to separate ya jaw from ya skull!" he jabbed back.

My amazing friend was loud, opinionated, direct, half-joking, and exactly who God intended for me to talk to. This brother-in-Christ and dear friend is a man I call when I need reminding of who

God is and who I am in Him.

"All jokin' aside, bro. I want to ask you to do me a favor?" He paused. "I want you to lead our Bible study on Friday. I know that is when your team prays, but I know my team needs a different voice in the darkness, B."

"Sure, but are you guys going to be working?" I questioned.

"We are labeled an essential service by the government. We are still running calls like crazy. Just trying to run to the shops in shifts to keep everyone away from each other. It's crazy. My office team are like air traffic control trying to keep everyone from crashing, and those folks are my prayer machines right now," he quickly replied.

"But how do you want me to do the Bible study?" I questioned.

"Oh, we all got computers and tablets so I will send you a webinar invite. Isn't that how you are doing business today?"

"Oh, yeah we are." I cleared my throat.

"Good!" he exclaimed. "I mean, God told us GO and make disciples, not go make pretty buildings and the people will show up, huh? Okay, Friday it is! Love ya, gotta run now." He hung up the phone.

As my smart phone went silent, the scripture my friend quoted reverberated through my spirit. These are moments where, my friends and family will tell you, I have only one phrase to say: "You can't make this stuff up." My friend's comment forced me to return to the scripture I had read dozens of time. He was right. There were no restrictions on how we are to "go." I can "go" and "make disciples" without ever leaving my house. I was trapped in my own needs to "go," not in the unrestrictive arms of my Savior. I was reminded, in that brief conversation, that God does not need me to "go" anywhere to use me. He can save the world in dreams, manifestations, or voices in the wind should he choose. However, he chooses each man and woman of God to be his hands and feet, and he placed each of us directly inside our "go" moment. Even if we are trapped inside our own issues or quarantined by life, His plans remain true. If we grab this truth, a revival will start and cascade into generations to come.

"Surely the arm of the Lord is not too short to save, nor his ear too dull to hear." Isaiah 59:1

When Friday came around, I clicked on the link my friend sent me. I had prepared a short and concise devotional and flipped my yellow note pad back and forth semi-nervously. However, to my amazement, when I logged onto the webinar, there were twenty-five employees already logged into their computers or devices. I greeted everyone, and my friend gave me a quick introduction. My hands began to sweat. I asked my friend to open us in a prayer. As his voice boomed through the computer speakers, I stopped my video and muted my computer to say a quick prayer of my own. "Papa, this has to be you, not me. Do what only you can do. Amen."

With a rocky start and a few technology issues, I thundered my way through the scriptures I had prepared. Then God led me to simply speak into the fear surrounding our nation and world. As I shared my honest concerns and how I was struggling, I could visibly see faces on the screen change. Almost immediately the team, through the webinar, started asking questions and opened up more freely about their own fears. The honest conversation quickly turned into "Where do we cast our fears?" or "Where do we turn when we are afraid?" With the devotional time ending, I told the team Jesus is the only true cure for our fear and that he repeatedly tells us not to fear in his word. I asked if anyone wanted to surrender their lives to Jesus for the first time. Three men quickly responded into their devices.

After the webinar ended and I told the men to connect with my friend, I logged off amazed. I stood dumbfounded and asked Papa-God to continue to destroy the boxes that I had put him inside. I realized, in that devotional, that I needed him to retrain and re-teach me. The world is telling me that I have lost control and I need to look out for myself. But when I lean into God, I realize that I was never in control—He is.

In just a few short minutes my friend called. His voice was surprisingly shaky.

"Brandon, this is it. This is what we are called to do. If we will come to a place in our lives where no matter the situation or circumstance we just want more of Jesus, then he will move. Today, those men got something the world cannot give them. Salvation. No matter how bad it gets or whatever comes next, God is going to do whatever he wants to do. Quarantine, no quarantine—you cannot stop the move of God from the hearts prepared for God. This is it, B. This is how God turns darkness into light. I have been working on these guys for two years and today it was either stay in fear or know the God that says, 'Fear not.'"

My friend was right. Can we control pandemics or fear? No. Do we still need to listen to warnings, wisdom, and cautions? Absolutely. However, do we hide our light under a basket? Never. For the world to be changed and business revival to break open, it starts in small ways like this. We must stop stockpiling our Sunday sermons and knowledge of God inside our hearts and offices. We must look beyond our daily numbers, duties, and requirements. Who will reach the remote employees? We send missionaries to the remote regions of the world, but who is empowering and sending their employees to the remote workers and tele-commuters?

I believe more deeply now than ever before the time is now to press into God – inside our businesses. There are millions of Christian missionaries who have been sent out into the workforce during this time. They are called church members. What if we started praying for God to open doors with our friends and colleagues? What if we started praying for God to expose deep fears and anxieties inside our employees? What if we made it a habit to "check-in" on our employees and then offered a listening ear or a heart-felt prayer?

The most beautiful thing I have realized during this strange new reality is that I serve a God who won't be shaken or denied by quarantine. We have a duty to love and serve the people under our leadership and in our workplaces. The people around us are the mission field God has laid at our feet. We must stop hording our "treasures" and faith for Sundays and Bible study groups. Even if we have never "led" someone to Jesus, we can pray for God to give us an opportunity to simply share our stories. We can start small: "How are you dealing with the fear?" Have you ever asked your colleagues to simply tell you their stories? The revival can start at any point. You are already inside the lives of people God is waiting to touch because you are inside the way they provide for themselves and potentially their families. Just like a missionary traveling to a foreign land, you have learned the language of your company. You know the local culture inside the walls. Connections have been made. All that is left to do is bring Your Jesus into this space. He will do the rest.

This is the time to be an ambassador for the Kingdom of God. Where you go, where your webinar takes place, who you pray for— there the kingdom of God goes! There are literally millions of embers around the globe waiting for a gentle breath of fresh air to ignite a business revival. Will you be a spark? Re-think the possible, because with God nothing is impossible.

"We are therefore Christ's Ambassadors, as though God were making his appeal through us...." 2 Corinthians 5:20

CONCLUSION

I resonate with Simon Peter more than any other disciple. He displays the most amazing moments in the Gospels as well as some of the most boneheaded. He witnesses miracles, walks on water and yet also denies Christ—after first cutting off a man's ear. This is the type of leadership needed for a business revival. It's not about perfection, but rather a commitment to pressing forward. Once our men and women of God realize they have been sent by God to the place where they work...a movement will begin.

Nothing illustrates this point more to me than the story found in Matthew 17:24-27.

> *After Jesus and his disciples arrived in Capernaum, the collectors of the two-drachma temple tax came to Peter and asked, "Doesn't your teacher pay the temple tax?" "Yes, he does," he replied. When Peter came into the house, Jesus was the first to speak. "What do you think, Simon?" he asked. "From whom do the kings of the earth collect duty and taxes—from their own children or from others? "From others," Peter answered. "Then the children are exempt," Jesus said to him. "But so that we may not cause offense, go to the lake and throw out your line. Take the first fish you catch; open its mouth and you will find a four-drachma coin. Take it and give it to them for my tax and yours."*

I point out this story for one major reason. When Jesus wanted to catch a fish with a coin in its mouth, he sent a fisherman. Jesus used Peter in his area of expertise, but He was the One who performed the miracle. Peter just fished and waited for God to bring the breakthrough. More times than I can count, I have seen God show himself mighty in the thing that I think I am already great at. I believe this is a major key to setting a fire in our world like never before. God wants to show us how to catch fish using the skills we already have, but He will be the One working a breakthrough. The business revival will begin when doctors are catching doctors, stay-at-home spouses are catching stay-at home friends, sales professionals are catching sales professionals, teachers are catching teachers, plumbers are catching plumbers, electricians are catching electricians, and lawyers are catching lawyers.

Inside our profession, we are working in a place where everyone speaks the same language. We spend forty or more hours a week with our co-workers: this is a place to see a lasting impact. What if the people placed in the office, truck, van, patrol-car, or cubicle were placed there specifically for you to pour Jesus into their lives and families? So many times, we get discouraged and daydream about going on a mission trip to the other side of the world, when maybe the mission is the office next door, little league field, co-worker, or playdate?

Wherever you are right now, I want you to picture yourself standing in front of a massive church congregation. The senior pastor calls you to the stage. You and anyone else connected to your life walk to center stage. The pastor places a confident hand on your shoulder and addresses the packed auditorium.

Today, we have the privilege of sending out Missionaries into the lands completely foreign to most of this whole congregation. As a matter of fact, this leader in our congregation has spent years learning the local language, spending time with the locals, and even learning all their customs. My great friend here will be traveling to their full-time job, and they need our prayers today. Reach out a hand in support of my dear friend here and pray as if you were going into the hostile environment. We don't know how long this leader and his family will be on the mission set before them, but we know they are going to make an unbelievable impact for Jesus.

Lead where you are...Love where you are...and the mission takes care of itself.